THE DUTCH IN THE MEDWAY

The DUTCH *in the* MEDWAY

P. G. ROGERS

New Foreword by J. D. Davies

Seaforth
PUBLISHING

TO
JHR. IR. CAREL MOLLERUS AND MEVR. AN MOLLERUS
IN TOKEN OF
AN ANGLO-DUTCH FRIENDSHIP

Copyright © Oxford University Press 1970

This edition first published in Great Britain in 2017 by
Seaforth Publishing,
A division of Pen & Sword Books Ltd,
47 Church Street,
Barnsley S70 2AS

www.seaforthpublishing.com

The Dutch in the Medway was originally published in 1970. This reprint is published
by arrangement with Oxford University Press.

British Library Cataloguing in Publication Data
A catalogue record for this book is available from the British Library

ISBN 978 1 4738 9568 3 (HARDBACK)
ISBN 978 1 9570 6 (EPUB)
ISBN 978 1 4738 9569 0 (KINDLE)

Printed and bound in Great Britain by CPI Group (UK) Ltd, Croydon, CR0 4YY

Contents

List of Illustrations

Foreword

The Dutch in the Medway, first published in 1970, was prompted by the tercentenary, three years earlier, of the Dutch attack in 1667. The author, Philip George Rogers, was not a historian, but he was a Man of Kent by birth, had served as a Major in the Intelligence Corps during the Second World War, and subsequently worked in the Foreign Office. He wrote a number of other works with a Kentish theme, such as a history of Gillingham, an account of the nineteenth-century Jezreelite sect which built a bizarre tower on Chatham Hill, and a study of the curious skirmish in Bossenden Wood in 1838, often described as the last 'battle' fought on English soil. Rogers also wrote history on a national scale, notably a study of the seventeenth century radical religious sect, the Fifth Monarchy Men, and a survey of Anglo-Moroccan relations to 1900 (a work financed by the Moroccan embassy in London, the British Moroccan Society, and Rogers' employer, the Foreign and Commonwealth Office).

The Dutch in the Medway, though, remains his most important and enduring work. Rogers cultivated an extensive range of connections in the Netherlands, and this contributed to the exemplary range of source material, from both British and Dutch archives and publications, which he used in the book. Rogers' other great strengths are his lively, easily accessible writing style, and his intimate knowledge of the local geography and of the tidal conditions in the Medway; an incidental bonus is the valuable little account which the author provides of the nature of, and local attitudes towards, the tercentenary commemorations in the Medway area in 1967. Almost universally well reviewed at its first appearance, the book is still by far the best and most detailed account in English of one of the pivotal events of the Stuart age, an event which, by common consent, also constitutes one of the worst defeats in British military and naval history. Naturally, the episode that the Dutch call the tocht naar Chatham – the jolly-sounding 'trip to Chatham' – has attracted rather more positive attention in the Netherlands, where it is rightly regarded as one of the defining triumphs of the Dutch 'golden age'. Even so, many Dutch histories published within the last twenty or thirty years cite Rogers, rather than any of their own works, as the standard account of the remarkable action fought in the Medway in June 1667. The republication of *The Dutch in the Medway* in a modern edition to mark the 350th anniversary of the Dutch attack should, therefore, be widely welcomed by historians and interested readers on both sides of the North Sea.

J D Davies
November 2016

Preface

As a man of Kent by birth and upbringing I have always had a
strong affection for the River Medway, particularly since some of
the happiest days of my boyhood were spent sailing on its waters,
from the Nore at its mouth to Allington Lock, high up the river
near Maidstone.

In those times, the years following the First World War, the
Medway was still largely unspoilt. The hideous oil refinery on the
Isle of Grain had not yet marred the entrance to the river; and the
Port Victoria Hotel, shuttered and silent but strangely elegant, a
forlorn relic of the spacious pre-war days, could still be seen on the
north shore where the tankers now tie up. On the opposite side of
the Medway, off Sheerness, battle-cruisers were often anchored,
with smaller ships of the Royal Navy near to them and adding
diversity to the scene.

Further up the river, beyond the two nineteenth-century forts,
Hoo and Darnett, which guarded the entrance into Gillingham
Reach, lay Upnor Castle and Chatham Dockyard, and in these
upper reaches destroyers and other small warships were for years
after the war laid up in pairs, giving the river in those parts an
unusually crowded appearance. Barges, with gaily painted upper-
works and beautiful russet sails, were still numerous, and where
the fairway was narrow and congested one often passed within
yards of them and exchanged pleasantries with the skippers, or
abuse if doubt was cast on one's ability to navigate.

The river had indeed many delights to offer, and these could be
enjoyed at a very modest price by embarking on one of the
paddle-steamers which plied during the summer months from
Strood and Chatham Piers, taking trippers on day-excursions to
Sheerness and Southend. The greatest enjoyment, however, came
from piloting one's own small boat on the Medway; and this I

was able to do in full measure, since I belonged to a troop of Sea Scouts. On one memorable occasion we decided to stage, with the modest nautical resources at our disposal, our own version of the Dutch raid in the Medway in June 1667. We divided the troop into two sections, and one, representing the English, departed in their whalers up-river for Upnor Castle, whilst the other, representing the Dutch, remained at Gillingham. At a pre-arranged time both sections set sail and met, as far as I remember, half-way down Cockham Wood Reach. Here a spirited engagement took place, in which bags of soot and flour were freely used as ammunition, until the battle had to be ended as supplies had run out.

I forget who were judged to have won in this encounter—but the memory of it, long dormant, was reawakened when I read in 1967 that plans were being made in the Medway Towns to commemorate the tercentenary of the Dutch raid. This commemoration duly took place; but one thing, so it seemed to me, was lacking. Though numerous articles have appeared, both in England and the Netherlands, on the Medway raid of June 1667, no book has been written which attempts to put it in historical perspective. I thought this was a task well worth undertaking, and the result is the present book.

I should like now to record my thanks for all the help which I have received while carrying out my researches, both in the Netherlands and in England. In the first place I am deeply grateful to my dear friend Jacques Plieger, formerly of the Royal Netherlands Navy, who has given me the benefit of his wide knowledge of maritime matters, and has helped me in many other ways in the preparation of this book.

I am also grateful for their assistance to: Captain A. R. Meyer of the Royal Netherlands Navy (retired); Lieutenant P. M. Bosscher, Royal Netherlands Navy, of the Helders Marinemuseum, Den Helder; Professor Dr. J. H. Kernkamp; Dr. M. A. P. Meilink-Roelofsz, and Dr. O. Schutte of the Eerste Afdeeling, Algemeen Rijksarchief, The Hague; Dr. P. Scherft, Director of the Zeeland Archives; Dr. L. M. Akveld; Dr. J. van Lohuizen, of the Library of Amsterdam University; Drs. J. R. Bruijn; Drs. E. Bos-Rietdijk, Curator of the Maritiem Museum 'Prins Hendrik', Rotterdam;

Mr. J. Braat and Mr. J. B. Kist of the Afdeeling Nederlandse Geschiedenis, Rijksmuseum, Amsterdam; Mr. M. Claes, Librarian of the Nederlandsch Historisch Scheepvaart Museum, Amsterdam; and Mevr. De Hoop-Scheffer of the Rijksprentenkabinett, Amsterdam.

In England, my thanks are due to Mr. A. W. H. Pearsall, Custodian of Manuscripts in the National Maritime Museum, Greenwich; and to Mr. A. G. Yates, Industrial and Amenities Administrative Officer, Borough of Queenborough-in-Sheppey. The two maps were drawn by Mr. Raymond Hyatt, to whom I am specially indebted for the patience he showed in face of constant requests for modifications. I also acknowledge with gratitude the permission given by the authorities of the Bodleian Library, the National Maritime Museum, the National Portrait Gallery, and the Rijksmuseum, Amsterdam, to reproduce items from their collections as illustrations in this book.

Finally I must add a note about the chronology I have used. In England in the seventeenth century the Julian Calendar (Old Style) was used. This was ten days behind the Gregorian Calendar (New Style) used by the Dutch and many other European countries. In this book I have adhered to the Old Style, and where I have used Dutch sources I have altered the dates to bring them into conformity with the Old Style.

12 April 1969   PHILIP ROGERS

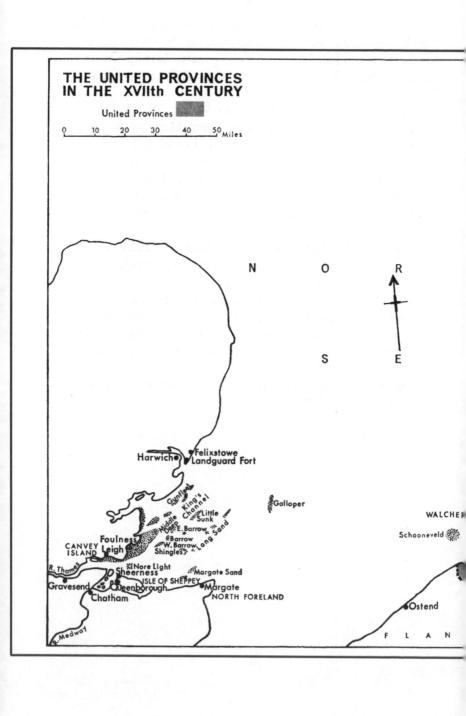

THE UNITED PROVINCES
IN THE XVIIth CENTURY

United Provinces

0   10   20   30   40   50 Miles

N   O   R

S   E

Harwich● ●Felixstowe
        Landguard Fort

●Galloper

WALCHER

Schooneveld

Gunfleet

King's Channel

Middle Deep
●Little
Sunk

Foulness
●E. Barrow
Barrow
W. Barrow
Shingles
Long Sand

CANVEY
ISLAND   Leigh

R. Thames

●Nore Light
Sheerness
Gravesend●   ISLE OF SHEPPEY   ●Margate Sand
        Queenborough   Margate
Chatham   NORTH FORELAND

●Ostend

R. Medway

F   L   A   N

TERSCHELLING

VLIELAND

TEXEL
Den Helder

H

Scheveningen
The Hague

Mouth of
the Maas
Brielle
evoetsluis
REE

AND

R   S

The Vlie

GRONINGEN

FRIESLAND

DRENTHE
(Provincial status only
recognised in 1796)

ZUIDER

ZEE

OVERYSSEL

Amsterdam

GELDERLAND

UTRECHT

C L E V E

Rotterdam   *R. Waal*

R. Rhine

Breda

THE GENERALITY

Venlo

R. Maas

East Scheldt

BISHOPRIC

OF

LIEGE

Maastricht

JÜLICH

Antwerp

R. Schelde

B R A B A N T

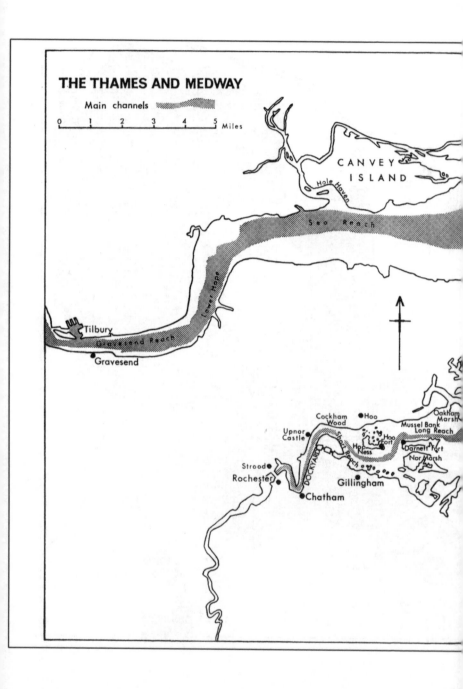

THE THAMES AND MEDWAY

Main channels

0   1   2   3   4   5 Miles

CANVEY ISLAND

Hole Haven

Sea Reach

Lower Hope

Tilbury

Gravesend Reach

Gravesend

Cockham Wood

Hoo

Oakham Marsh

Mussel Bank

Long Reach

Upnor Castle

Hoo Fort

Darnett Fort

Hoo Ness

Nor Marsh

DOCKYARD

Strood

Rochester

Gillingham

Chatham

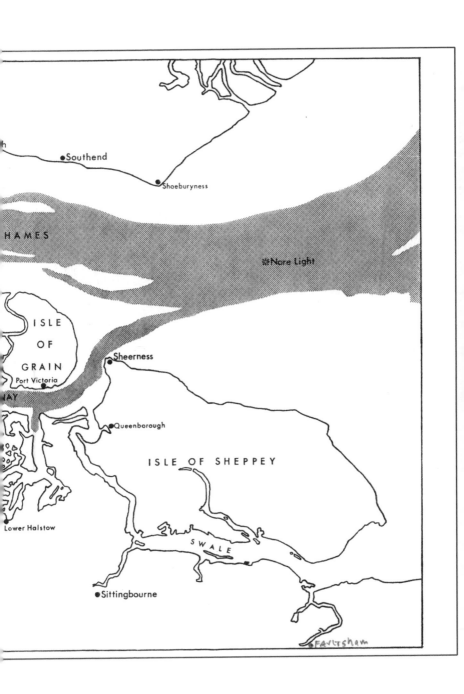

CHAPTER I

The Pismires of the World

IN 1671 a book was published in London under the title *The Present State of the United Provinces of the Low Countries*. The author, who inscribed himself as 'W.A., Fellow of the Royal Society',[1] had this to say in his preface:

Scarce any subject occurres more frequent in the discourses of ingenious men, than that of the marvellous progress of this little State, which in the space of about one hundred years (for 'tis not more since that first attempt to shake off the Spanish yoke) hath grown to a height not only infinitely transcending all the ancient Republicks of Greece, but not much inferior in some respects even to the greatest monarchies of these latter ages.

'W.A.' was not exaggerating when he thus described the astonishing rise of the United Provinces in the seventeenth century. In the Middle Ages the Low Countries had become the centre of a cloth-weaving industry which with its associated crafts brought into existence flourishing towns which came to be ruled by powerful burgher oligarchies. These towns formed part of various fiefs ruled over by counts and other feudal dignitaries, most of whom owned allegiance to the Holy Roman Emperor. In the late Middle Ages these fiefs had formed part of the Burgundian domains, but had come into the possession of the House of Habsburg through the marriage of Maximilian of that House with Mary, the heiress of Charles the Bold of Burgundy in 1477. In the early sixteenth century Maximilian's descendant the Holy Roman Emperor Charles V rewarded Philibert, Prince of Orange, a small principality in the South of France, with extensive possessions in the Low Countries. Philibert died without issue, and his possessions

---

[1] The initials concealed the identity of William Aglionby.

and titles came ultimately to the House of Nassau in Germany, into which his sister had married. Thus was established the line of Orange-Nassau, which was to play such an important part in the meteoric rise of the United Provinces to power and prosperity in the seventeenth century.

The Holy Roman Emperor Charles V abdicated in 1555 and his son Philip II of Spain inherited his possessions in the Low Countries. Philip precipitated a conflict with his subjects there by introducing unpopular measures infringing local liberties and the powers of the nobility, and above all by his determination to stamp out Protestantism. In January 1579, after many years of inconclusive struggle, the provinces of Holland, Zeeland, Gelderland, Friesland, and Utrecht (joined later by Groningen and Overijssel) and with the towns of Ghent, Bruges, Antwerp, and Ypres, formed the Union of Utrecht for mutual support, to maintain their ancient rights and privileges, including the right to choose the kind of religion they wished to follow. In May of the same year, however, the southern provinces of the Netherlands, predominantly Catholic, made their peace with Philip II, and so the northern provinces in the Union of Utrecht were left to continue the struggle alone, without the support of the rich and powerful towns in the South.

From this union of seven provinces was born a new nation, the United Provinces of the Netherlands. It was in effect a federation of small sovereign republics, each of which had its own 'States' or assembly, representing the burgher aristocracy of the towns and the landed nobility. These local 'States' guarded jealously the sovereign rights of the provinces, but they sent representatives to a central assembly called the 'States-General', which dealt with affairs affecting the federation as a whole, and appointed the leaders of the armed forces. The centre of gravity of the federation lay, however, in the province of Holland, where the major towns of Amsterdam, Rotterdam, Delft, Dordrecht, and Leyden were situated, and which therefore played a preponderant part in the trade and political and cultural life of the federation. The degree of importance was reflected in the titles by which the States-General, the States of Holland, and the States of the other provinces came to be addressed. The States-General were 'their High Mightinesses', the States of Holland 'their Noble Great Mightinesses', but the States of the remaining provinces simply 'their Noble Mightinesses'.

The assassination of William the Silent at Delft in July 1584 was a terrible blow to the cause, but the motto of his House, 'Je maintiendrai', which had been exemplified by his courage and tenacity, was not betrayed by his successors. At this critical period help came from England, for Queen Elizabeth sent an army to support the rebels, and after many vicissitudes the Spaniards were obliged to sign a truce of twelve years' duration in 1609. The struggle was resumed, however, when the truce expired in 1621, and it was not till January 1648 that Spain signed a peace treaty in which she acknowledged the sovereign independence of the United Provinces.

Thus after nearly a century of unremitting and heroic struggle the Dutch had won their freedom. But no sooner had the conflict with Spain ended than they found themselves faced with what, in the end, was to prove a much more formidable rival—England. The basic cause of the rivalry was that both countries were maritime States, and competitors for trade not only in European waters but also all over the world. One of the most remarkable features of the Dutch struggle for independence was that, whilst fighting for their very existence at home, they nevertheless managed to build up an extensive foreign trade and found an empire. This, however, was undeniably due not only to their own inherent industry and initiative, but also to a combination of circumstances in the early seventeenth century which proved favourable to them. Spain was gradually worn down by her struggle with England, and then with France. France herself was hampered by the war of the nobles against the Crown which is known as the War of the Fronde (1648–55); and England was preoccupied for six years (1643–9) with her Civil War. Again, the Thirty Years' War (1618–48) which laid the German lands waste and involved the maritime Powers of the north, also gave the Dutch much more scope to extend their trade and overseas possessions.

3

Moreover, throughout the latter years of the Dutch struggle for independence four English and two Scottish regiments formed an indispensable part of the army of the United Provinces. These troops were recruited by permission of the British monarch, whose subjects they remained, though, being in Dutch pay, they also took an oath of allegiance to the States-General. The acquisition of such a considerable fighting force greatly eased the strain felt by a small country on whose manpower the sea made such demands.

Nevertheless, despite the conjunction of favourable circumstances, it remains an extraordinary achievement of the Dutch, that whilst they were fighting for their existence as a separate State, they were able to make that State the leading commercial and colonial Power of the seventeenth century. The foundation of this achievement was, prosaically, the humble herring. At the end of the fourteenth century a method of preserving herrings had been discovered, and these cured or pickled herrings became a valuable trade commodity. The herrings abounded in the North Sea, and periodically made their way in vast numbers down the east coast of Scotland and England from the Orkneys southwards. The Dutch gradually developed a very well organized and efficient 'Great Fishery' to gather in the rich herring harvest, and a considerable number of the people of the province of Holland in particular came to be directly dependent on the Great Fishery for their livelihood.

The Dutch sold the herrings, packed in barrels, or exchanged them in return for other goods, and they built up a strong connection with the Baltic States in particular. From this trade they obtained the timber, tar, hemp, and other such maritime necessities which enabled them to build up a great merchant fleet, become the carriers of Europe, and develop their naval power. In shipbuilding the Dutch showed great ingenuity based on practical experience, in the construction of different types of vessel, and one of their greatest achievements was the introduction of a three-masted merchant ship known as the *fluit* (fly-boat). This type of vessel, easy to handle and thus needing a comparatively small crew, was developed at the end of the sixteenth century, and proved invaluable to the Dutch as an auxiliary transport in their fighting fleets because of its great carrying capacity.

The development of the shipbuilding industry and the creation of a strong fleet, coupled with the native hardihood and maritime instincts of the Dutch, led to the foundation of overseas colonies and trading posts around the world; and these further reinforced the might and prosperity of the tiny republic of the United Provinces. In 1602 the Dutch East India Company was founded, and from Batavia in Java, its headquarters, a colonial empire was developed in the Far East by such great men as Jan Pietersz. Coen, who became Governor-General of the Company in 1617. The trading posts and settlements in the Far East, with the rich commerce which they engendered, contributed immeasurably to the power and prosperity of the United Provinces, but other ventures, too, helped to extend the overseas might of the mother country. The Dutch took Ceylon and established themselves on the Malabar and Coromandel Coasts of India; while in 1652, in order to have a port of call on the voyage to the East Indies, they settled at the Cape of Good Hope.

The seamen and merchant adventurers of the young republic were equally enterprising in establishing trading posts in Africa, on the West Coast around the Gulf of Guinea, and also in the New World, across the Atlantic. In 1614 they established a small settlement on Manhattan Island at the mouth of the Hudson River; in 1616 they began their occupation of territory which later became Dutch Guiana; and in 1621 their West India Company was founded. All these developments threatened to bring them into conflict with the English, particularly their settlement at the mouth of the Hudson River, which challenged English claims on the east coast of North America.

Dutch maritime and commercial expansion was accompanied at home by a flowering of the arts and sciences which made the United Provinces, during their golden age in the seventeenth century, a centre of civilization from the achievements of which other less enterprising countries were not slow to draw benefit. There was indeed hardly a sphere of human activity of which the Dutch, at this time, were not the leading exponents. In shipping, trade, and finance they were supreme, and have indeed been described as 'the economic schoolmasters of seventeenth-century Europe'.[1] In knowledge and application of the mechanized sciences, also, they had no equals, and their practical ability was reflected in the skills which they brought, for example, to land-drainage and reclamation, and the building of ships. In the realm of scientific invention they produced such men as Christian Huygens, famous for his researches on the refraction of light, for his optical instruments, and his invention of the spiral spring in watches. Hardly less famous was van Leeuwenhoek, the microscopist, and indeed the debt the world owes to him, and other well-known contemporaries, is incalculable.

The maritime enterprise of the Dutch led to the emergence of some renowned map-makers, including Wagenaer, who produced sea-charts which were used extensively not only by the Dutch themselves but by other sea-faring nations. These Dutch charts were in such common usage in English ships, indeed, that they came to be known as 'Waggoners', the nearest the English could get to the Dutch pronunciation. Another great Dutch cartographer of the seventeenth century, Blaeu, produced maps which were not only useful but beautiful too, and as works of art they command high prices today in the salerooms.

In philosophy this golden age of the Dutch produced Spinoza, in political science Grotius, whose great work *De Jure Belli et Pacis*, published in 1625, entitles him to be considered one of the founders, if not the father, of international law. In literature, too, a sphere in which the Dutch have in general not excelled, the seventeenth century produced some great figures, notably Joost van den Vondel, whom the Dutch consider to be their greatest poet. It was, however, in the seventeenth-century school of Dutch painting that the civilization of the United Provinces reached its apogee. Masters such as Rembrandt, Cuyp, Hobbema, Ruysdael, Jan Steen, to mention only a few, reflect and focus in their genius the magnificent upsurge of a small nation of less than two million people, whose multifarious activities and achievements made them the exemplars of their age.

[1] R. H. Tawney, *Religion and the Rise of Capitalism*, London, 1944, p. 204.

No neighbouring country was more affected and influenced by the Dutch in the seventeenth century than England. This was inevitable, partly because of the proximity of the two peoples but also because of the many affinities, such as their economic and maritime interests, which connected them closely. England's ties with the Low Countries had been strong in the Middle Ages, when English wool was the staple export, sent across the sea to be made up into cloth by the skilled weavers of the Netherlands. In the reign of Elizabeth close links had been forged with the rebels in the northern provinces, because of the common opposition to Spain. During Elizabeth's reign, too, many emigrants fled from the Netherlands to begin new lives away from Spanish persecution; and English troops fought to help save the rebellious seven provinces in the north from being subdued by Spain. After the immigrants who had fled from persecution came others who entered England to better themselves economically; for in comparison with the United Provinces England was a backward country which afforded greater opportunities to enterprising Dutchmen than did their own country, where competition was keener.

The close ties between England and the United Provinces resulted in an ever increasing Dutch influence as the seventeenth century progressed. Dutchmen such as Cornelis Vermuyden helped to drain the fens; others played a leading part in mining, printing, and other industrial activities; while the popularity of the Dutch formal garden and architectural styles, notably the use of the gable, also reflected the pervasive spread of Dutch influence. The connection between the two countries was reinforced when in 1641 William, the only son of Frederick Henry, and grandson of William the Silent, married Mary, the daughter of Charles I and Henrietta Maria. Thus was inaugurated a link between the Houses of Orange and Stuart which was to have important effects on the history of both countries at various times in the seventeenth century.

It might well be supposed that because of the many ties between England and the United Provinces their relationship would be friendly. The reverse was the case, however; and even before the

7

end of the reign of Elizabeth envious voices began to be raised in England against the neighbour over the sea. The root cause of the growing jealousy was maritime and commercial rivalry; and the English sought to justify their envy of the Dutch by asserting that the English monarchs had exclusive dominion over what were vaguely described as 'the British seas'. Learned treatises were written purporting to prove that such a dominion had existed since the time of King Alfred, at least, if not before; and attempts were made with a wealth of misapplied erudition to justify the English pretensions, for which there was, in fact, very little basis. It is true that at various times during the Middle Ages English kings had ordained that foreign vessels should lower their sails when ordered to do so by the king's admiral or lieutenant at sea. This regulation was made to enable supervision to be maintained over peaceful commerce, by forcing ships to halt for inspection. Nevertheless, from the application of this purely police measure, a tradition arose that foreign warships should lower their topsails and strike their flags when they met an English man-of-war in the Narrow Seas.[1] To avoid trouble foreigners usually complied, but when they did so they considered that they were merely performing an act of courtesy, and not acknowledging a prescriptive right of the English to dominion of the seas.

In England, however, all kinds of precedents were quoted in an endeavour to prove that what was a courtesy was in fact a right. There was a traditional story, which was still circulating in the reign of Charles II, that even Philip II of Spain, when sailing to England to marry Queen Mary, had been forced to order the commander of his ship to strike his flag to an English ship. The Spaniard, so the story went, had at first refused to strike his flag, so the English ship had fired a shot. This penetrated to King Philip's cabin, and induced him to order that the flag should be struck. Afterwards he complained to Queen Mary about the incident, but she was said to have replied that if the English captain had acted otherwise than he did he would have answered for it with his life.[2]

In the early seventeenth century the pre-eminence of the Dutch

---

[1] The English and Irish Channels.
[2] Calendar of State Papers Domestic (C.S.P.D.), 1668–9, pp. 363–4.

in the North Sea herring fishery led James I to revive the doctrine of the sovereignty of the seas, as a justification for measures which he took to limit the Dutch fishermen. In 1609 he issued a proclamation which declared all the fisheries along the coasts of the British Isles to be royal preserves, and foreigners were forbidden to fish within them without first obtaining a licence from the king.

Because of the proclamation a dispute began between the English and Dutch which, since it affected a vital sector of the economy of the United Provinces and was for the English a question of prestige, proved hard to settle. Attempts by James I and Charles I to make the Dutch pay for the right to fish in the North Sea met, understandably, with opposition on the spot and with strong protests from the Dutch Government, as did any assertion that the striking of the flag to an English warship was not a mere act of courtesy, but recognition of English dominion over the Narrow Seas.

Though the English found Dutch predominance in the North Sea fishery economically distasteful and an affront to national pride, the enterprise and vigour with which the Dutch faced them as competitors for overseas trade and possessions caused even more jealousy and ill-feeling. The rivalry was world-wide—in North America, the Caribbean, West Africa, India, South-East Asia, and Japan—but it was at its keenest, perhaps, in the rich spice islands of the East Indies, which the Dutch East India Company wished to keep as its own exclusive preserve. This policy led to frequent clashes with the ships and traders of the English East India Company, and a particularly ugly incident occurred in 1623 on the island of Amboyna in the Moluccas, which the Dutch had taken from the Portuguese in 1605, and which was a centre of the trade in cloves. In 1615 the English had set up a trading post on the island, and this was still in being in 1623, when the Dutch accused the English traders of conspiring with the natives against them. In accordance with the general practice of the time the accused men were tortured to extract confessions, and nine of them were afterwards executed. This affair, which came to be known in England as the massacre of Amboyna, embittered Anglo-Dutch relations for many years, until at last a settlement was reached at

9

the end of the first Anglo-Dutch war in 1654, involving the payment of compensation by the Dutch. For many years after that,
however, the memory of Amboyna continued to afford a convenient pretext for exacerbating feelings against the Dutch.

In England animosity against them was enflamed because of the
role which they played as middlemen in European commerce. For
example, a good deal of the English imports from the Baltic
States and from southern Europe did not come directly from the
countries of origin, but by way of the United Provinces, which,
owing to Dutch maritime enterprise, had grown into a huge
entrepôt of trade. Moreover, such was the preponderance of Dutch
shipping, a large proportion of the imports were actually brought
into England in Dutch vessels. The Dutch even benefited from
native English industry, particularly from cloth manufacture. For
want of skilled workers in the finishing processes English cloth
had to be exported in large quantities to the United Provinces,
where it was dyed and otherwise made ready for the market. In
the reign of James I an attempt was made to develop the export of
finished cloth in England; but this led to Dutch counter-measures
which seriously affected the English industry, and led to increased
bitterness between the two countries.

The worsening of relations was reflected in books and broad-
sheets, the contents of which often reached incredible depths of
scurrility. Sir William Monson, who had been an English vice-
admiral during the reign of Charles I, wrote a number of tracts
dealing with naval affairs, and in some of these he referred with
envy and hatred to the Dutch. One of his tracts was entitled: *A
Discovery of the Hollanders' Trades, and their circumventing us therein,
and the Means how to reduce the Fishing into our hands, as of Right due
to us.* In the tract Monson declared: 'It is manifest that fish has
brought them to a great strength both by land and sea . . . let us
labour to follow their example.' He went on to assert: 'Our eyes
and senses make it clearly appear that they [the Dutch] and their
cunning courses are the immediate causes of the poverty that daily
assails our glorious kingdom.' After further diatribes, however,
Monson's honesty forced him to pay a tribute, though grudgingly,
to the Dutch:

Though I have made a description at large of the Hollanders' inconstancy, faithlessness, and manifest injuries they have offered to us, yet I must say there is no man so wicked or vicious but some kind of virtue will appear in him, for which he deserves cherishment, as well as chastisement for the other. But, naturally, they are people that desire rather to live without virtue than to die without money, and this that followeth shall set forth their praises in the worldly carriages. They are frugal in expense . . . they are industrious . . . just in contracts, holding a conscience, in the little religion they have, not to defraud any man. They labour and seek out the secrets of lands not inhabited and countries undiscovered. They are inventors of arts, which, to their praise, they have enriched the world with.[1]

A favourite theme of English pamphleteers was the alleged ingratitude of the Dutch for all the help which the English had given them during their struggle for independence. In 1652, for example, a pamphlet appeared in London with the title: *A Seasonable Expostulation with the Netherlands, Declaring their Ingratitude to, and the Necessity of their Agreement with, the Commonwealth of England.* In this the writer told the Dutch that '. . . A foot of ground cannot be called yours, that owes not a third part to the Expense, Valour and Counsell of the English.'

In the same year another pamphlet appeared under the following title: *A Brief Character of the Low Countries under the States, being three weeks observation of the Vices and Vertues of the Inhabitants.* The writer of this pamphlet resorted to much abuse. The United Provinces were, he declared, 'the great bog of Europe'; and as for the people, they were 'generally boorish . . . without doubt very ancient, for they were bred before manners were in fashion'. He went on to assert: 'You may sooner convert a Jew than make an ordinary Dutchman yield to arguments that cross him.' Yet this writer, like so many others who were ill-disposed to the Dutch, felt bound to pay tribute to their qualities:

Almost all among them are seamen born, and like frogs can live both on land and water. . . . They are the pismires of the world . . . the storehouse of the whole of Christendome . . . making by their industry all the fruits of the vast earth their own.

[1] M. Oppenheim (ed.), *The Naval Tracts of Sir William Monson*, Navy Records Society, Vol. V, pp. 227, 241, 303, 325.

English propaganda against the Dutch reached a very low level in a pamphlet which appeared in 1653, and which was entitled: *The Dutch-mens Pedigree or A Relation, Shewing how they were first Bred and Descended from a Horse-Turd, which was enclosed in a Butter-Box*. 'Out of which dung,' said the writer, 'within nine days space sprung forth men, women and children: the off-spring whereof are yet alive to this day, and now commonly known by the name of Dutchmen.' The writer maintained this level of abuse throughout the pamphlet, which ended thus:

Do not wonder that the Dutch have acted so hellishly like devils as they have . . . do not wonder at their wicked, traiterous and unjust wringing of all trade out of other men's hands: nay, do not wonder at their barbarous and inhumane cruelties, since from Hell they came, and thither without doubt they must return again.

The Dutch-mens Pedigree appeared during the first Anglo-Dutch war of the seventeenth century, which explains the viciousness of its attack. The rivalry between the two States was such that a conflict was inevitable, given the temper and economic theories of the times; and that it did not break out before it actually did, in 1652, was due to a large extent to the weakness of England under Charles I. When under the Commonwealth the emphasis on English trade and maritime interests became more pronounced, and, what was more to the point, a powerful fleet was brought into being to defend and further them, a war with the Dutch was bound to follow.

In January 1651 the States-General had agreed to recognize the English Commonwealth, and the English Parliament decided to send a special mission to propose what amounted to a political union between the two republics. The envoys arrived at The Hague in March 1651, but received an unfriendly reception from the populace, who were backed up by English royalist refugees shouting abuse such as 'executioners!', 'regicides!', and 'Cromwell's bastards!' The negotiations between English and Dutch lasted into June, but proved abortive. The Dutch refused the proposal for a close association because they feared it would entail the subordination of the United Provinces to England; and this refusal, coupled with English resentment over the insults to which their envoys had been subjected by Orangists and the English royalists at The Hague, caused Parliament to veer to the other extreme, and led to the passing of the Navigation Act in October 1651. Under its provisions exports from England were to be carried only in English ships, while imports were to be brought either in English ships or ships of the country which produced the goods.

This blow aimed at their vital carrying trade caused the Dutch to send a mission to London in December 1651 to try to negotiate a peaceful settlement even at the eleventh hour. But, as the prospect of a successful issue of the discussions lessened, both English and Dutch sent their fleets to sea as a precautionary measure, and war became inevitable, when, in May 1652, a dispute occurred in the Straits of Dover between an English squadron under Blake and the Dutch fleet under Tromp, over the time-honoured question of whether the Dutch should salute the English flag in the Narrow Seas.

Even after this incident the Dutch envoys remained in London, but they were finally recalled at the end of June, and at the beginning of July war was formally declared. After two years of fighting at sea, during which honours were fairly evenly divided—although the Dutch lost their great admiral Tromp—peace was made by the Treaty of Westminster in 1654. By this the Dutch agreed to recognize the Navigation Act, and to salute English ships in the Narrow Seas, though no mention was made in the treaty that such saluting constituted an acknowledgement of England's pretensions to dominion over the Narrow Seas. This ambiguity led to further trouble in the future, as did another clause of the treaty of peace, under which the Dutch agreed to pay compensation for any wrongs proved to have been inflicted on English merchants in the past, in the East Indies. In short, the Treaty of Westminster did not mark the termination of the Anglo-Dutch struggle in the seventeenth century, but only the end of the first phase. Further bitter conflicts lay ahead.

CHAPTER II

The English and Dutch Affairs

ONE OF THE most interesting aspects of Anglo-Dutch history in the seventeenth century is the similarity between political developments in the two countries. In each there was a dynasty supported by the nobles and also enjoying support from time to time and for various reasons from the 'lower' classes, or from sections of them. In the United Provinces the dynasty was the House of Orange, in England the House of Stuart, and these came to be closely connected by marriage and thus established in some respects a community of interests.

The seventeenth century also saw in each country the rise of a powerful wealthy middle-class, its fortunes based on trade and commerce, whose aspirations soon brought it into conflict with the older aristocratic class whose fortunes were founded on land ownership. In England this conflict between the Crown and landed aristocracy on the one hand, and the rising middle class on the other, contributed towards bringing about the Civil War. Though a struggle of such dimensions did not take place in the United Provinces, the antagonism between the Orangists and the burgher middle class led to intermittent upheavals which played a decisive part in the shaping of events.

The powerful town oligarchies in the various provinces, especially those in the leading province of Holland, formed a close-knit community whose interests were based on their maritime and commercial activities. These burghers tended to favour a policy of peace (though not peace at any price), because war disrupted trade and therefore their business. It must be emphasized, however, that they did not constitute a broad-based 'democratic' group in the modern sense of the word, for the ordinary Dutch working people had little if any share in the government of the towns, and as little say in the activity of the various provincial assemblies.

In contrast with the policy favoured by the burgher element in the United Provinces, the princes of the House of Orange tended to follow a policy which was not exclusively based on mercantile considerations but in which, for example, dynastic interests played a part. For this and for other reasons the Orangists and the 'States-Party' or 'Republicans' (the community of interests of the burgher oligarchies) came intermittently into collision. At such times the Dutch working classes, or at least sections of them, were inclined to support the Orangists, not necessarily because they identified themselves with the dynastic interests of the Princes of Orange, but because they hated the wealthy middle-class mercantile oligarchies who strove to keep all power within their hands.

In 1647 Frederick Henry, Prince of Orange, died, and was succeeded by his son William II who had married Princess Mary of England. He opposed the peace with Spain made in 1648, which had been carried through largely by the determination of the powerful States of Holland. Moreover he naturally favoured the Stuart cause in the English Civil War, whereas the burgher classes, particularly in the province of Holland, were more sympathetic towards the parliamentary cause. In the summer of 1650 relations between William and the States of Holland deteriorated sharply, but in November he died suddenly of smallpox,[1] and the States of Holland took advantage of the circumstances to inaugurate a peaceful but revolutionary change of government in the United Provinces.

A special 'Grand Assembly' of representatives of all the provincial States was convened at The Hague in January 1651 at the request of the States of Holland, and this assembly abolished the office of Stadholder and the associated positions of Captain-General and Admiral-General of the armed forces. These posts had been held by the Princes of Orange in the past, and had helped

---

[1] His only son, William, was born a week after his death and became later William III of England.

to give them great power and authority. As a result of the changes agreed on in the 'Grand Assembly', however, much greater scope was given to provincial particularism, and because of the pre-eminence of the States of Holland the *Raad-Pensionaris* of that assembly became, for the next twenty years, the most important person in the Government of the United Provinces. The title of this functionary, literally translated, means 'Council Pensionary', the word 'pensionary' having the sense of 'paid official'. The *Raad-Pensionaris* presided over the meetings of the States of Holland, acted as secretary with regard to all the written records and correspondence, and above all was Holland's chief representative in the States-General. Since Holland was so preponderant in the federation of the United Provinces, a capable *Raad-Pensionaris* would be able without much difficulty to assume the chief role in the conduct of the country's affairs.

Such a man was Johan de Witt, born in Dordrecht in 1625, who became *Raad-Pensionaris* of Holland in July 1653, and is known to the English by the free rendering of his title as the 'Grand Pensionary'. It is no exaggeration to say that de Witt was a political genius; and his gifts were demonstrated by the success he achieved in the difficult tasks of managing the different factions within his country, and of dominating the complicated international scene in pursuance of Dutch interests. Inflexible will-power and determination marked his policy of refusal to compromise on what he considered to be vital national interests. Sir William Temple, who knew de Witt well, wrote of him: 'This maxime running through his whole frame: that a State is at an end, when they are brought to grant the smallest matter out of fear, or to offer at purchasing any alliances otherwise than by mutual interests and reciprocal advantages.'[1]

Another English contemporary, Bishop Burnet, who also knew the United Provinces and the Dutch well, said of Johan de Witt: 'For the administration of justice at home, and for the management of their trade, and their forces by sea, he was the ablest minister they ever had.'[2]

[1] D. Jones, *Letters Written by Sir William Temple*, London, 1699, p. 23.
[2] Thos. Burnet (ed.), *History of His Own Time*, London, 1809, Vol. I, p. 309.

De Witt was no lover of the House of Orange. His father, burgomaster of Dordrecht, had been one of six deputies of the States of Holland whom William II Prince of Orange had arrested in 1650 and incarcerated in the castle of Loevestein for having disbanded troops without the consent of the States-General. In 1654, therefore, when the treaty of peace was signed with England which brought the first Anglo-Dutch war to a close, de Witt raised no objection to a secret agreement with Cromwell by which the States of Holland undertook never to appoint any member of the House of Orange as Stadholder or Captain-General of the United Provinces. When news of this secret agreement ultimately leaked out, relations between the Orangists and the burgher party naturally became exacerbated.

Another stipulation of the peace treaty made in 1654 was that Charles II should not be allowed to remain in exile in the United Provinces; he had come there after the parliamentary victory in the Civil War, to be near his relations at The Hague. This undertaking too, for obvious reasons, de Witt did not find unpalatable, and so the unfortunate Charles was forced to leave his more or less agreeable haven at The Hague. This was an experience which he never forgot, and it strengthened his support of the Orange party and his detestation of de Witt and the Republicans.

In March 1660, when his fortunes turned at last, Charles was in Brussels; but acting on advice in a letter from General Monk in England he crossed into the United Provinces, and here he was given an effusive welcome by the States-General; the members shrewdly foresaw the inevitability of his restoration to the throne of his ancestors. Charles was invited to The Hague, and there he was shown the utmost deference and sumptuously feasted. On 15 May a squadron of ships from England arrived at Scheveningen under Admiral Montagu,[1] who flew his flag in the *Naseby*, one of the fine ships built for the Cromwellian fleet. The king boarded the *Naseby* on 23 May for the return voyage to England; but before she set sail she was renamed the *Royal Charles* in honour of the occasion. At dawn on Friday 25 May the squadron reached Dover, and after a triumphant progress to London Charles at last

---

[1] Created Earl of Sandwich in July 1660.

entered into his own on Tuesday 29 May, by a happy coincidence his thirtieth birthday.

After all the celebration was over, one of the many problems awaiting the king's attention was that of Anglo-Dutch relations. Charles had no reason to feel friendship towards the republican oligarchy who controlled the policy of the United Provinces, despite their belated overtures to him when his restoration had proved imminent. However, commercial and maritime rivalry still dominated the relationship between the two countries, so that some accommodation was necessary if peace was to be preserved.

During his reception by the States-General before he left for England, the deputies had assured Charles of their unfailing esteem and expressed a wish for close and friendly relations between the two countries. Replying in the same vein, Charles had solemnly affirmed his love for the Republic and his desire to live in peace and amity with it.

The result of these mutual professions was that a Dutch delegation arrived in England in October 1660 empowered to negotiate a treaty between the two countries. No sooner, however, had the discussions begun than all the old causes of disagreement came to the fore again. The Amboyna affair was raked up, the right of the Dutch to fish without permit off the British coast was firmly rejected, English rights to freedom of trade in the East Indies were equally firmly asserted, and lastly no compromise was said to be possible on the Navigation Act, which was in fact re-enacted in strengthened form in 1660.

In view of the dismal prospect which these difficulties portended, the Dutch later proceeded to reinsure themselves by making an alliance with France. Under this treaty, which was concluded in April 1662, the United Provinces and France contracted to help each other in maintaining their possessions, rights, and privileges, and agreed that if either country were attacked by a third Power, the other should declare war on the aggressor within four months.

A few months later, in September 1662, an Anglo-Dutch treaty was also signed, but it fell far short of the expectations which both parties had originally entertained, and the fundamental causes of Anglo-Dutch rivalry remained. For example, though by Article

X the Dutch agreed to salute the English flag in the Narrow Seas as had hitherto been the custom, no mention was made that this would imply recognition of the English claim to sovereignty of the seas. Again, Article XV, which dealt with the island of Pularoon, lying south-west of New Guinea in the Banda group, was a compromise which really pleased neither Dutch nor English. The latter had settled in Pularoon, a centre of the nutmeg trade, in 1616, but had been forced to leave by the Dutch, anxious as ever to preserve their monopoly of trade in the Spice Islands. Under the Treaty of Westminster (1654) the Dutch had agreed to surrender Pularoon, but had failed to do so; now, under Article XV of the new treaty, they reluctantly undertook this. It was stipulated, however, that the island should be handed over only on condition that the many claims of the English East India Company for compensation for damages and wrongs allegedly suffered at the hands of the Dutch should be waived up to the year 1659.

The essence of the situation after the return of Charles to England in 1660 was that in each country a powerful mercantile interest was determined to preserve what advantages it already possessed, and to extend its trade and overseas connections wherever possible. Both de Witt and Charles were associated with these wealthy and influential middle classes, and through self-interest took their views into consideration when framing policy. In London there was a power-group consisting of the wealthy City merchants and various leading personalities of the Court, who had a financial interest in the ventures sponsored by the City. For example, in December 1660 a charter was granted to a company called 'The Royal Adventurers into Africa'. Members of the royal family including the Duke of York and Prince Rupert, and prominent men such as the Duke of Albemarle and the Earl of Sandwich were shareholders, and King Charles himself undertook to subscribe £6,000, though this money was never paid.

The purpose of the company was to open up trade with the West Coast of Africa, but as the Dutch were already firmly established there, and determined to resist any encroachments from the English or any other outsiders, trouble was bound to occur. The first venture of the company was under command of Robert

Holmes, a pugnacious and able leader, who had served during the Civil War in the royalist army and then, like so many of his contemporaries, had turned to the sea and proved as capable a commander on water as on land. He arrived off the Gambia in March 1661, and after taking possession of an island at the mouth of the river which he named Charles Island, he captured a fort on another island higher up, which he named James Island. The Dutch claimed this island and fort as their territory, and Holmes' actions evoked strong protests from the States-General. Clashes with the Dutch along the West Coast of Africa inevitably followed, and in November 1663, therefore, another squadron was sent out under Holmes to defend the company's possessions and, so his instructions read, to promote its interests. Holmes carried out these duties with his customary vigour, and took or destroyed a number of Dutch ships and posts in the process.

Across the Atlantic, the presence of the Dutch in their colony of New Netherlands at the mouth of the Hudson River was a constant irritation to Charles II, and in March 1664 Captain Richard Nicolls was put in charge of an expedition which was to sail to New England and there concert measures for the capture of the Dutch settlement. To lend colour of legality to the project Charles, with sublime indifference to the fact that the Dutch had been settled in the New Netherlands for many years, granted to his brother James, Duke of York, lands on the North American seaboard which included the area of Dutch settlement. Nicolls sailed from Portsmouth in May 1664, reached New England in late July, and at the end of August forced the Dutch to surrender New Amsterdam, capital of New Netherlands. Later, in honour of James, it was renamed New York.

As soon as news of Holmes's exploits reached them, the Dutch made vigorous protests against an expedition the conduct of which seemed to them indefensible in view of the fact that England and the United Provinces were formally at peace. This was undeniable, and to save Charles's face, Holmes was sent to the Tower of London on his return in January 1665, to await the results of an inquiry into his actions. He was, however, released in March without punishment or reproof and indeed received a pardon for any offences which might have been committed. The reason for this leniency was that Holmes had maintained that he was forced to take extreme measures because of the recalcitrance of the Dutch and their refusal to parley; and in face of the prevailing state of tension such a defence could not but be successful.

Meanwhile the Dutch had not contented themselves solely with making representations. De Witt had dispatched de Ruyter with a small squadron to re-take the forts which Holmes had captured in West Africa and most of these de Ruyter did regain for the Dutch. Then he sailed across the Atlantic but his squadron was not strong enough to make an attempt to recapture New Amsterdam so he sailed back to the Netherlands. His return was most welcome to his fellow-countrymen, because the transition from undeclared to formal war between England and the United Provinces had now occurred.

The disposition of the English ambassador at The Hague, Sir George Downing,[1] was not such as to encourage hopes that peace might be preserved by negotiation. Downing had been a loyal supporter of Cromwell and in 1657 had been appointed English representative at The Hague, a post which he occupied till 1660. In April of that year, sensing the inevitability of the restoration of Charles to the throne, he sought and obtained the king's pardon, and Charles, who realized his importance as an expert on Dutch affairs, later knighted him and dispatched him once more to The Hague in 1661.

Downing seems to have been a person of singularly unpleasant character. Pepys likened him to a 'perfidious rogue', and Lord Chancellor Clarendon, more austerely, called him 'a man of proud and insolent spirit'. Bishop Burnet was no less uncomplimentary and affirmed that Downing was 'a crafty, fawning man'. Burnet also said that when Downing was sent as ambassador to The Hague the Dutch 'had reason to conclude he was sent over with no good intent, and that he was capable of managing a bad design, and very ready to undertake it'.[2]

---

[1] Downing is remembered now chiefly because of the street in Whitehall named after him, in which he occupied a house which later became the official residence of the Prime Minister.

[2] *History of His Own Time*, Vol. I, p. 278.

Some idea of Downing's character and methods of work can be gleaned from what he himself told Pepys, as the latter recorded in his diary on 27 December 1668. According to Downing, during his stay in the United Provinces he had organized such an efficient private espionage service that he had often

had the keys taken out of de Witt's pocket when he was a-bed, and his closet opened and his papers brought to him and left in his hands for an hour, and carried back and laid in the place again, and keys put into his pocket again.

Downing may have had some unpleasant personal traits but in economic and financial affairs he was an acknowledged expert; this enabled him to negotiate skilfully and tenaciously with the Dutch—who also prided themselves, not without reason, on their economic and financial acumen—over matters of dispute arising from the Anglo-Dutch treaty of 1662. Downing did not like the Dutch, and showed no willingness to compromise in his dealings with them. His dislike was heartily reciprocated; de Witt regarded him almost as an *agent provocateur* and a major contributory cause of the worsening of Anglo-Dutch relations.[1]

Downing's failure to achieve a settlement of matters in dispute arising from the 1662 treaty, and the continuation of sporadic clashes on the high seas between English and Dutch were accompanied in England by the reappearance of anti-Dutch pamphlets and books. For example a book was published in 1664 entitled *The English and Dutch Affairs Displayed to the Life*. In his preface the writer declared:

Here hast thou truly presented (and not in a Multiplying Glass) the great Kindnesses the Dutch have from time to time received of the English; and on the other side, how unthankfull the Dutch have been for them. . . . If thou beest a True English-Man, thou canst not but in reading it very much rescent the Injuries and Affronts which the English have continually received from that Nation.

Having presented this picture of English benevolence and base Dutch ingratitude, the writer proceeded to re-hash all the old causes of quarrel, paying particular attention to such events as the Amboyna 'massacre'. His points were made by other writers, and

[1] *The Works of Sir William Temple*, London, 1720, Vol. II, p. 42.

the same thesis of alleged Dutch ingratitude was expounded in Thomas Mun's *England's Treasure by Foreign Trade*, also published in 1664. Mun bluntly accused the Dutch of taking the bread out of Englishmen's mouths through their herring fishery in the North Sea and their attempt to monopolize the rich trade with the Far East.

These and similar strictures were of course well received, particularly in the City of London, and in April 1664 some of the merchants there sent a petition to the House of Commons. They alleged that the Dutch had obstructed their commerce, had captured their ships, had attacked their trading settlements, and in fact had caused them enormous loss for which they now claimed compensation. Parliament received the complaint sympathetically and in a joint resolution of both Houses Charles II was asked to take steps to ensure that the Dutch ceased their nefarious practices forthwith and refrained from interfering with English trade in the future. The matter was referred to Downing at The Hague, and so one more item was added to the long list of controversial issues which were the subject of bitter and protracted debate between that pugnacious negotiator and the Dutch.

Despite the mounting clamour for war emanating from the City merchants and their friends and fellow-shareholders at Court, Charles II had considerable reservations about the wisdom of such a policy. These did not arise from any feelings of tenderness towards the Dutch, for whom he had no particular personal liking, but because he presciently feared the effects on the monarchy which the financial strain of a war might involve. His chief minister, Lord Chancellor Clarendon, fully shared these doubts.

Meanwhile the Dutch, fearing the worst, were prudently preparing and strengthening their naval forces, and in December 1664 the States-General decided to build no fewer than twenty-four new men-of-war as a reinforcement of the fleet. In England too, despite Charles's and Clarendon's hesitation, the will to make ready for an armed struggle was evident. In February 1665 the House of Commons voted the sum of £2,500,000—a huge allocation for those times—to be spent on strengthening the fleet and on other war preparations.

23

Shortly afterwards the formal declaration of war was made on the United Provinces, who for their part had already declared war in January 1665. This had followed an attack by an English squadron under Admiral Thomas Allin in December 1664 on a fleet of Dutch merchant ships off Cadiz. The Dutch considered this latest episode in the mutual campaign of reprisals too flagrant to be condoned, though the English sought to justify it as a retribution for de Ruyter's recent campaign against the English in West Africa and the West Indies.

The war between England and the United Provinces which followed, the second Anglo-Dutch war of the seventeenth century, was to be fought mainly at sea, for maritime and commercial supremacy. In 1609 the Dutch jurist Hugo Grotius had published his *Mare Liberum* (Free Sea) in which he pleaded for freedom of navigation in all the seas and oceans of the world. *Mare Clausum* (Closed Sea), written by the English jurist John Selden and published in 1635, was on the contrary a defence of the English argument that the 'British Seas' could not be unconditionally free to the navigation of all nations, because of the English monarch's alleged traditional right to dominion over them.

Neither the English nor the Dutch were logical in this controversy over *Mare Liberum* and *Mare Clausum*. The Dutch, for example, wanted freedom in the North Sea because of their herring fishery but insisted on restriction in their overseas preserves, particularly in the East Indies. Similarly the English upheld *Mare Clausum* in home waters, to exclude Dutch competition, but claimed *Mare Liberum* abroad, wherever they penetrated in search of trade and found the Dutch already there. Basically, therefore, the second Anglo-Dutch war was the result of determination by the mercantile interests in both countries to interpret the theory of *Mare Liberum* and *Mare Clausum* elastically, as it best suited their own purposes.

CHAPTER III

The Navy Ript and Ransackt

IN ANY MARITIME and commercial struggle with England the Dutch suffered one fundamental disadvantage, which arose from their geographical situation. The British Isles lay athwart their lines of communication with the oceans of the world; and if, being at war with England, they wished to reach these oceans, they had either to risk the narrow passage through the English Channel, or else send their ships on a long circuitous voyage around the north of Scotland, where again English men-of-war might be lying in wait to intercept them.

In addition, however, to this grave natural disadvantage the Dutch effort at sea was always liable to be weakened by a lack of centralized direction. This resulted from the existence of no fewer than five separate admiralties—a defect which was due to the particularism of the provinces, and the federal structure of the State. The province of Holland had three of these admiralties, the first of the Maas, at Rotterdam, the second of Amsterdam, and the third of what was called the 'Noorderkwartier' (the northern part of the province). The two remaining admiralties, which were extremely jealous of their separate existence and prerogatives, were of Zeeland and Friesland.

The rivalry among these admiralties often hampered the Dutch war effort, unless a strong hand was at the helm to call them to order; and sometimes the determination of one admiralty not to be outdone by another led to almost ludicrous results. For instance, it was a point of honour that the leading naval officers of one admiralty should not be inferior in rank to those of the others. Thus a promotion in one was likely to be followed soon afterwards by promotions in the others, leading to a superabundance of flag-officers. Owing to this practice a Dutch fleet which put to sea in 1665 under command of Van Wassenaer van Obdam included no less than twenty-one officers of flag rank: lieutenant-admirals, vice-admirals, or rear-admirals. It is not difficult to imagine the jealousies and friction which this state of affairs could lead to when the fleet was at sea.

Nevertheless the Dutch more than neutralized the disadvantages under which they laboured by their unremitting efforts to create a strong fleet of well-found ships, manned by crews whose conditions of service were made as favourable as possible. They fed their seamen well, in the light of the standards of the age, they paid them regularly, and they looked after their dependants should need arise. Partly because of these comparatively good conditions, but also because of the limited opportunities ashore, the Dutch (unlike the English) never needed to press men into the sea service. Indeed they usually found that numerous foreigners, Englishmen amongst them, were willing to volunteer for employment in Dutch ships.

In the mid-seventeenth century the energetic all-pervading influence of the Grand Pensionary Johan de Witt was an important contributory factor to the maintenance and strengthening of Dutch naval power. Not the least of this remarkable man's many qualities was a percipience in maritime matters which was based on actual service at sea with the fighting ships. During his leadership special deputies for naval affairs appointed by the States-General were perpetually going the rounds of the admiralties to ensure that order and efficiency were maintained in the dockyards and in the ships of the fleet, and in this way, too, some check was imposed on provincial jealousies.

The first Dutch war with England, in 1652-4, had revealed imperfections in the Dutch fleet, and de Witt and the States-General determined to remedy these. A big shipbuilding programme was put in hand, and this reached a peak in 1665, when the *Zeven Provinciën* (ninety guns, 420 men, built in Delfshaven for the Admiralty of the Maas, and later to gain renown as de Ruyter's flagship) was launched. Because of the naval programme, when the formal stage of hostilities between England and the

United Provinces began in the early months of 1665, the Dutch were already on a war-footing, and well-prepared with a strongly-manned fleet. This comprised some hundred vessels in all, mounting 4,800 guns, and with crews totalling 21,000 men.

The same could hardly be said of England, whose fleet and naval administration had experienced since the death of Queen Elizabeth some amazing vicissitudes. Under the queen's successor James I the administration of the navy had suffered at the hands of incompetent and corrupt officials, and its effectiveness declined still further under Charles I, though in this reign the prime cause of decay was the king's chronic shortage of money. Under the Commonwealth, however, a change for the better occurred. This was largely due to the fact that for the first time for many years sufficient money was made available for the fleet. This money came from various sources such as the sale of royalists' lands, and while it lasted new ships were built, and the conditions of the seamen improved by regular payment of wages, supply of better food, and care of sick and wounded. However, as funds one by one dried up, a naval debt gradually accumulated again during the latter years of the Commonwealth and Protectorate, and conditons became bad again.

In 1649 Parliament had abolished the traditional title and office of Lord High Admiral, and substituted a committee whose members came to be known as the Commissioners of the Admiralty. Likewise Parliament had abolished the Navy Board, the small group of officials known as the 'Principal Officers of the Navy', whose origin went back to the reign of Henry VIII, and which was responsible for the administration of the navy. In place of the Navy Board Parliament established a small group of Navy Commissioners, and these, together with the Admiralty Commissioners, supervised the thorough reorganization of the navy in Cromwellian times which enabled it to meet the Dutch on equal terms in the first Anglo-Dutch War, and give such firm backing to Cromwell's foreign policy. A fine fleet was brought into being through an ambitious building programme, and in 1649–51, for example, forty-one new ships were added to the fleet, and these were continuously added to. In 1654 this rebuilding programme reached its peak when no fewer than twenty-two new men-of-war were launched.

The creation of the parliamentary fleet, and the improvement in the conditions of the seamen who manned it, cost a great deal of money; in fact during the Commonwealth more than half the national revenue was spent on the Navy. There were, however, other demands on the revenue, for example for the upkeep of the large army kept in being by Cromwell. As hitherto available sources of money gradually dried up the naval administration began once again to suffer from lack of funds, and the old abuses, such as failure to pay the seamen regularly, began to creep back. Moreover, a naval debt was accumulating. In February 1660, just before the restoration of Charles II, the arrears of pay owed to seamen amounted to £400,000, and some of the men had been unpaid for four years. The total naval debt had risen to an estimated £1,284,452, so that the unfortunate Charles II inherited a naval deficit which was to prove a fatal handicap.

However, when he returned to England the future of the fleet seemed to be assured. Both Charles himself and his brother James, Duke of York, were deeply interested in naval affairs, and frequently visited the dockyards and ships of the fleet. Charles, as well as James, knew enough about the sea and ships to be able to hold his own in discussions even with experts. The king's specialized knowledge earned him a curious tribute from Bishop Burnet, who wrote: 'He understood navigation well; but above all he knew the architecture of ships so perfectly that in that respect he was exact rather more than became a Prince.'[1]

As for the Duke of York, in 1638, when he was only five years old, his father Charles I had made him Lord High Admiral of England for life. When he entered into the full exercise of the office after the restoration of Charles II, James soon proved by his enthusiasm and diligence in every branch of naval affairs that he regarded his position not as a sinecure, but as a post of honour and responsibility, which he was determined to fill to the best of his ability. In this he succeeded; and as Bishop Burnet remarked of him, 'he came to understand all the concerns of the sea very particularly'.[2]

[1] *History of His Own Time*, Vol. I, p. 128.   [2] Ibid., p. 237.

These concerns included active command of the fleet at sea, as well as a meticulous supervision of the administration of the Navy on shore, so that the new naval administration which Charles installed after his return to England in 1660 suffered no lack of direction from above. At the time of the Restoration naval affairs were being supervised by a number of Admiralty Commissioners whom the Rump Parliament had appointed after its return to Westminster in 1659. These commissioners had under them another smaller group of men versed in maritime affairs, whose task (like that of the former Navy Board and its successor the Navy Commissioners) was to see to the day-to-day administration of the fleet and dockyards. Charles II did away with both these bodies, and in their place he revived the office of Lord High Admiral and restored the old Navy Board. The men he appointed to this latter body, who were known as the 'Principal Officers of His Majesty's Navy', were Sir George Carteret, Treasurer; Sir Robert Slingsby, Comptroller (succeeded on his death in 1661 by Sir John Mennes); Sir William Batten, Surveyor; and Samuel Pepys, the diarist, Clerk of the Acts.

Pepys, whose job was to keep the records and act as secretary to the Board, knew a little about the sea and ships but almost nothing about naval administration at the time of his appointment. This he had obtained through the influence of Edward Montagu, Earl of Sandwich, to whom he was distantly related. Montagu had taken Pepys with him in the *Naseby* when in May 1660 he had sailed for Scheveningen to bring Charles back to England, and for Pepys this had been a memorable experience. When appointed Clerk of the Acts, he applied himself with enthusiasm to his new duties, and in addition to the secretarial work which was involved, gradually made himself master of the details of naval administration to such an extent that he became an indispensable member of the Navy Board, and the channel through which its activities flowed.

In addition to the Principal Officers three commissioners were also appointed to the newly constituted Navy Board. These were Lord Berkeley, Sir William Penn, and Peter Pett. In 1662 William Coventry (knighted in 1665) was appointed as an additional commissioner, and soon proved his worth by his diligence. He had been secretary to James Duke of York since 1660, and so had acquired an extensive knowledge of naval administration which stood him in good stead and made him a valuable reinforcement of the Navy Board. In 1664 yet another additional commissioner was appointed: Lord Brouncker, the first President of the Royal Society and a close friend of the diarist John Evelyn. Brouncker also was assiduous in the performance of his duties, though he lacked the expert naval knowledge of men such as Coventry and Mennes.

Peter Pett, one of the three commissioners originally appointed in 1660, was made resident commissioner at Chatham Dockyard. He was a member of a family which by the time of the Restoration had been engaged in the building of ships for at least one hundred years, for a Peter Pett was building ships at Harwich, where the family settled, in the reign of Henry VIII. From Harwich Peter's descendants moved to positions as shipwrights in places on the Thames—Limehouse, Wapping and Deptford—and soon the name Pett became synonymous with the Royal Navy. The son of the Peter Pett who had built ships in the reign of Henry VIII was also called Peter, and he became Master Shipwright at Deptford, where he died in 1589. By his second wife this Deptford Peter had a son called Phineas, who became an assistant Master Shipwright at Chatham during the reign of James I, but was afterwards transferred to Woolwich. Phineas, who died in 1647, supervised the building of the famous vessel the *Sovereign of the Seas*, the largest and most decorated vessel of the fleet. This ship, which was of 1,637 tons burden, and carried 102 guns, cost with her embellishments the enormous sum of £40,833; and when she was launched at Woolwich in 1637 she was a tribute to the shipbuilding genius of the Pett family, for Peter Pett, the later resident commissioner at Chatham, had helped to build her under the direction of his father Phineas. A painting by Sir Peter Lely, which hangs in the National Maritime Museum, shows the stern view of the *Sovereign of the Seas*, with Peter Pett standing proudly by the side holding a pair of calipers in his hands (see Plate I).

Peter, the fifth son of Phineas by his first wife, was born at

Woolwich in 1610, and after serving as assistant to his father there for many years was made Commissioner of Chatham Dockyard in 1647. In this post he was responsible for all the dockyard activities, so that he had to exercise powers which far transcended those which he had formerly had as an assistant Master Shipwright. It was not as an administrator, however, but as a shipbuilder that Peter Pett impressed his contemporaries. John Evelyn, for example, commented in his diary on 2 August 1663:

Passing by Chattam, we saw his Majesties Royal Navy, dined at Commissioner Pets, Master Builder there, who shewed me his study and Models, with other curiosities belonging to his art, esteemed for the most skillfull *Naupagus* (i.e. shipbuilder) in the World. He has a pretty garden and banqueting house, potts, status, cypresses, resembling some villa about Rome...

In 1648, when a royalist rebellion broke out in Kent, Chatham Dockyard remained loyal to Parliament, although the rebels seized Upnor Castle and three men-of-war lying in the Medway. According to Peter Pett, in a report which he sent to the Admiralty Committee, it was he who had frustrated the royalists by denying them entrance into the dockyard, and by recapturing from them the three ships which they had taken.[1]

The position to which Pett had been promoted at Chatham was very important, for by the mid-seventeenth century the dockyard there had become the most important English naval base. It had risen to this eminence for a number of reasons. In the first place it was near to London, and therefore accessible for royal visits. Secondly, the Medway at Chatham was narrow and in other ways suitable for the building and repair of ships as carried out in the seventeenth century. Thirdly, Chatham lay near to the great wooded area of the Weald of Kent and Sussex, and this was a very important consideration, for the transport of the huge treetrunks needed in the construction of ships presented a major problem in an age of poor communications.

In the seventeenth century the natural advantages possessed by Chatham had been reinforced by strategical requirements. Because of the growing rivalry with the Dutch, there was a need for a

[1] Hist. MSS. Commission, *Portland MSS.*, Vol. I, pp. 459–61.

convenient harbour facing the North Sea, whence the fleet could sail with the minimum of delay towards the enemy coast. Again, a safe anchorage was needed near the Thames Estuary where the fleet could lie as a defence to the approaches to London. Chatham fulfilled both these strategic needs better than any other place, and contemporary writers on naval affairs recognized this. Sir William Monson, in the reign of Charles I, said: 'Chatham is so safe and secure a port for the ships to ride in that his Majesty's navy may better ride with a hawser at Chatham than with a cable at Portsmouth', and he went on to state:

The water at Chatham flows sufficiently every Spring tide to grave [clean] the greatest ships. No wind or weather can endanger the coming home of an anchor in Chatham, and the river affords sufficient space for every ship to ride without annoying one another. If Holland or the Eastland become our enemies, then doth Chatham lie most with our advantage to annoy them, if they attempt any part of our north coast, or Norfolk, Suffolk, Essex and Kent.[1]

The stages by which Chatham rose to its position of pre-eminence during the late sixteenth and seventeenth centuries can be traced in a series of measures beginning in 1547–50, when some storehouses for the use of the navy were hired or built at Gillingham, a little lower down the river. In June 1550 the Privy Council ordered that in future, when crews were paid off, the ships of the fleet were to be laid up or 'herbarowed' in the Medway off Gillingham. In August of the same year warships lying at Portsmouth were accordingly brought into the Medway and moored off Gillingham, preparatory to their being grounded for cleaning. The river at Chatham, however, proved to be more suitable for repairing and building ships, since it was narrower, and so there the dockyard came to be established. During the years 1570–84 storehouses were built at Chatham, a forge and mast-pond and graving-dock were constructed, and a house, called the 'Hill House', standing near St. Mary's Church and overlooking the river, was leased for the use of senior dockyard officials.

The dockyard was enlarged in the early seventeenth century, when new docks, wharves, storehouses, and mast-ponds were

---

[1] *The Naval Tracts of Sir William Monson*, Vol. V, pp. 5–7.

constructed, and a rope-yard was established. These additions, extending down the river bank, came to be known as the New Yard, to distinguish them from the earlier buildings in the vicinity of St. Mary's Church, which were called the Old Yard. The importance which Chatham acquired as a centre for the building and repair of ships, and the use of the Medway as an anchorage for the fleet, made the construction of defences essential. In 1560, therefore, work was begun on the construction of a fort at Upnor, on the opposite side of the Medway, and a little lower down the river from Chatham, so that it could guard the approaches to the dockyard. The fort was finished in 1564, and came to be dignified with the name of Upnor Castle. In 1575 another fortification was constructed at Swaleness, opposite Queenborough on the Isle of Sheppey, to hinder an enemy attempting to enter the Medway by way of the Swale; but this fort, unlike Upnor, was afterwards allowed to fall into decay. As for the ancient castle at Queenborough, this was demolished in 1650 as being not worth the cost of repair, since it was in such a ruinous state.

Upnor Castle was not considered to be a sufficient defence against a determined attack on the dockyard at Chatham, and so in 1585, at the suggestion of Sir John Hawkins, a chain was stretched across the Medway just below the castle as an additional protection. As another precaution, against a possible enemy attempt to avoid Upnor Castle by mounting an attack on the dockyard by way of St. Mary's Creek, instead of by the main channel of the Medway, the entrance to the creek had been blocked by piles in 1574.[1] Finally, in 1596, instructions were issued to ensure that on the approach of an enemy the dockyard officials at Chatham, and the garrison at Upnor, should have due warning and time to prepare the necessary counter-measures. It was laid down that a vessel should patrol constantly off Sheerness, and that if an enemy approached, this vessel was to warn a pinnace riding nearby. The pinnace had then to sail up the Medway to give the alert to Upnor Castle and Chatham Dockyard.

[1] St. Mary's Creek disappeared during 1862-85, when the dockyard was greatly enlarged by taking in St. Mary's Island. Three large basins were constructed where the creek had been, and these still separate 'St. Mary's Island' from the rest of the dockyard.

It is hardly an exaggeration, however, to say that during the seventeenth century the dockyard suffered more from corruption and inefficiency at home than from any damage inflicted by enemies from abroad. In the reign of James I the state of the naval administration was such that a commission of inquiry was appointed in 1608, and at Chatham Phineas Pett, assistant Master-Shipwright, was found guilty of many malpractices, including embezzlement of government stores. Probably because his expert knowledge as a shipbuilder made him indispensable he was not dismissed, and thus encouragement was given to men in less important positions to continue in corrupt practices.

In the reign of Charles I the conditions at Chatham were so bad that the dockyardmen marched in a body to London in 1627 in an endeavour to force the authorities to pay some of the arrears of wages due to them. The desperate state of the royal finances was also reflected in the fact that in the same year ships in dock at Chatham could not be repaired because there was no money available to pay for the materials required. Even during the Commonwealth, when for a time the purged naval administration functioned with vigour and efficiency, corruption continued at Chatham; and once again members of the Pett family were implicated.

In November 1651 two shipwrights in the dockyard wrote to the Navy Commissioners and informed them that there had been 'whisperings between honest men of grand abuses' at Chatham, and that the persons who knew about these abuses were frightened to disclose any details because of possible retaliation by the Petts. The writers of the letter declared that members of the family employed in the dockyard were, in fact, 'so knit together that the devil himself could not discover them, except one impeached the other'.[1]

The shipwrights' complaint about the Petts was repeated by William Adderley, who had been appointed during the Commonwealth to be resident preacher at Chatham, with the duty of giving sermons to the seamen and dockyardmen every Sunday in the sail-loft. Adderley seems to have conceived that his position as

[1] C.S.P.D., 1651–2, pp. 37–8.

moral guide necessitated an attempt to purge the dockyard of the corrupt practices which were rife; and so in November 1651 he petitioned for a commission of inquiry, stating that he had

observed much corruption, and tried to remedy it by speaking to the Commissioner on the place [i.e. Peter Pett] but he takes part with the offenders, and upbraids those who complain as meddlers, and smothers up abuses, his kindred being concerned therein.

Adderley emphasized the habit of the Petts to stand by one another in case of trouble, and he concluded that it was not in the country's interests to have 'a generation of brothers, cousins and kindred packed together in one place of public trust'.[1]

His petition contained such grave accusations that a commission of inquiry was indeed set up, and the members conducted their investigation in January 1652. The charges against Peter Pett, Commissioner of the dockyard, were that he had embezzled government stores; those against his brother Captain Phineas Pett, Clerk of the Check,[2] that he had not mustered the workmen, had entered more men as working than had actually been employed, had set down higher wages than those actually paid, and had pocketed the monies thus accruing. Another Pett, Peter's cousin Joseph, assistant to the Master-Shipwright, was also accused of embezzlement; and Richard Holborn, Master Mast-Maker, also a cousin of Peter Pett, was accused of stealing Government stores. Holborn was said to have had a bedstead made for himself from dockyard timber, and, with melancholy foresight, to have had two coffins made, which were taken to his house to be stored there to await the demise of himself and his wife.

Holborn and the Petts denied all the charges made against them, and Peter Pett counter-attacked by bringing accusations against Adderley, alleging that he had neglected to preach to the sailors and dockyardmen, and that he had, moreover, 'used ill language' and threatened to ruin the Petts. The upshot of the investigation was that in February 1652 it was decided that all the accused were to be retained in their employment; but it is not

[1] Ibid., pp. 41–2.
[2] An official who had charge of records of workmen employed, and wages paid, etc.

clear whether this decision was reached because the evidence
against them was not found convincing, or whether it was judged
unwise to dispense with their services at a time when relations
with the United Provinces were deteriorating so fast that war
seemed imminent. At all events Adderley also was retained as
preacher at Chatham, and it may be that he was regarded as a
useful watchdog to have on the spot to keep the Petts and other
officials in the dockyard up to the mark.

When Charles II was restored to the throne in 1660, Peter Pett
was allowed to continue as Commissioner at Chatham, despite
his loyalty to the Commonwealth and Protectorate. This was due
partly, no doubt, to his unrivalled ability as a shipbuilder, but also
to the services which he had rendered at the time of Charles's
return to England. Pett had been sent over with the squadron
under Montagu which sailed to Scheveningen in May 1660, and
Pepys recounted in his diary on 16 May that Pett had come aboard
the *Naseby* in order to 'get all things ready for the king'. He seems
also to have organized the embarcation from Scheveningen, for
Pepys noted on 20 May:

Commissioner Pett at last came to our lodging, and caused the boats to
go off; so some in one boat and some in another, we all bid adieu to the
shore. But through the badness of weather we were in great danger,
and a great while before we could get to the ship.

Pett's services at this time must have brought him to the notice
of the king, and he advanced a stage further in the royal favour in
1661, when he built a yacht for Charles. Pepys recorded in his
diary on 21 May 1661 that the king had sailed down the Thames
in the yacht that day, to test it, and that after the test it was considered to be better than a yacht which the Dutch had given to
Charles as a present. Nothing could have pleased Charles more;
and Peter Pett, the master shipbuilder, must have felt that his
position at Chatham was secure, since he had so gratified the king,
whose love of sailing was equalled only by his love of horse-
racing and dalliance with the ladies of the court.

Pepys, in his capacity as Clerk of the Acts, had much to do with
Pett, both socially and officially, but he did not allow social con-

tacts to cloud his judgement of Pett. As Commissioner at Chatham, the latter had charge of the 'Chatham Chest',[1] and had to render account periodically of his management. In his diary for 3 December 1662 Pepys recorded:

To Deptford; and so by water with Mr. Pett home again, all the way reading his Chest accounts, in which I did see things which did not please me; as his allowing himself £300 for one year's looking to the business of the Chest, and £150 per annum for the rest of the years.

Because of the large naval debt which Charles had inherited from the Commonwealth and Protectorate, the prospect of an improvement in the naval and dockyard administration after 1660 was poor, despite the appointment of a Navy Board which included some able and experienced men. Indeed, after 1660, because of the inadequacy of the financial settlement which was made at the Restoration, conditions in the navy and the dockyards deteriorated still further.

Parliament granted Charles the proceeds for life of various taxes; and these, together with other sources of income, and the hereditary revenues accruing to the Crown, were estimated to provide Charles with an annual sum of £1,200,000. This was supposed to be sufficient to enable him to carry on the government of the country. But even though Parliament later sanctioned further taxes and made special grants, the expected annual revenue of £1,200,000 was never realized; and in fact, usually only about two-thirds of this sum became available each year during the first part of Charles's reign. Even if the full £1,200,000 had been raised each year Charles would still have found it insufficient to meet all the multifarious expenditures involved in government. He was forced, therefore, to have resort to all kinds of desperate expedients, some of which, such as the farming out of taxes to corporations or rich individuals, or borrowing at excessive rates of interest, afforded temporary alleviation only at the cost of making matters much worse in the long run.

[1] The 'Chatham Chest' had been established in 1590 by Sir John Hawkins. It was a fund, built up by compulsory contributions deducted from seamen's pay, for the relief of the sick and wounded.

The effects of the chronic shortage of money were to be seen in every branch of the naval administration after 1660; and the State Papers, and writings of contemporaries such as Pepys and Evelyn, give some idea of the dishonesty, corruption, inefficiency, and decline of morale which the disastrous state of Charles II's finances inevitably brought in its train. On 6 December 1660, for example, Phineas Pett wrote from Chatham Dockyard to the Navy Board, stating that much government property such as timber and rope was being stolen. He recommended, therefore, that a watch-house should be built in the Old Dockyard to discourage thefts. Such practices continued at Chatham and other dockyards, however; and on 19 November 1661 a royal proclamation was issued, expressly to provide for the safeguarding of naval stores. It ordained that government property was to be marked wherever possible with a broad arrow or that, if this was not practicable, some other kind of identification was to be given it to deter pilfering.

The thieving which went on was due largely to the fact that the dockyardmen and the sailors often had to wait months, and sometimes years, before they received their pay, and therefore had to steal to keep themselves and their families alive. They did not receive their wages punctually because the Navy Board was usually without the necessary ready money; and for the same reason the officials of the Board found it more and more difficult to buy stores and provisions for the dockyards and the fleet. Contractors, understandably, had little faith in the Government's ability to pay, and from bitter experience were reluctant to grant credit. On 11 June 1661 Pepys stated in his diary that he and Sir George Carteret had resolved to write a letter to the Duke of York to inform him of 'the sad condition' of the Navy Board for want of money; how men would not serve without pay, and how the credit of the Board had been brought so low that 'none will sell us anything without our personal security given for the same'. On 31 July Pepys returned to the subject, noted that the navy was in 'very sad condition', and added, 'money must be raised for it'. On 31 August he complained that 'for lack of money all things go to rack' at the Navy Board; and again, on 30 September 1661, he

declared sadly that 'the want of money puts all things, and above
all the Navy, out of order'.

Several months later, on 28th June 1662, he wrote:

Great talk there is of a fear of war with the Dutch, and we have order
to pitch upon twenty ships to be forthwith set out; but I hope it is
but a scare-crow to the world, to let them see we can be ready for them;
though, God knows! the king is not able to set out five ships at this
present without great difficulty, we neither having money, credit, nor
stores.

John Hollond, who had spent many years in the naval administration, beginning in the reign of Charles I, wrote two *Discourses
of the Navy* (in 1638 and 1659), in which he expatiated on the
many abuses to which the service was subject. His second discourse, presented to the Duke of York, the Lord High Admiral,
in 1661, was entitled *The Navy Ript and Ransackt: or a Brief
Discovery of some few (of the many) Rents and Leaks of the Navy.*

In this work Hollond described at length the evils connected
with the payment (or rather non-payment) of wages, the embezzlement of stores, the corruption in the supply of victuals, and
all the other abuses of the naval administration. Pepys read
Hollond's discourses with great attention, and noted in his diary
on 25 July 1662: 'Much pleased with them, they hitting the very
diseases of the navy which we are troubled with now-a-days.'

The reluctance of contractors to give the Navy Board credit was
due to the fact that people who had done so in the past had gone
without payment for months, and in some cases years. On 4 April
1664 the case of some of these creditors was presented to Parliament. They had supplied goods valued at £140,000 which had
been used mostly to equip the ships sent over to Scheveningen in
May 1660 to bring Charles II back to England. But, Parliament
was told, the creditors had so far received no payment whatsoever
for the goods which they had supplied four years previously, and
this despite a resolution passed by the House of Commons on 13
July 1663 that they should be paid. The case of these creditors was
said to be grievous, some of them having been put in prison for
having failed to meet their own commitments, and their families
consequently being in great distress.

In February 1665, however, it seemed that the financial incubus which had lain so heavy and for so long over the navy would be removed. This was because of a special vote of £2,500,000 made by Parliament in that month to cover extra expenditure occasioned by war with the Dutch. But events were to prove that even such a large sum as this, allocated to enable Charles II to put the fleet on a war footing, was not sufficient to remedy the evils and repair the deficiencies which had prevailed for so long.

CHAPTER IV

Plague, Fire, and War

THROUGHOUT THE LATTER months of 1664 the Dutch and English were busy preparing their fleets for the war which both sides now realized was almost inevitable. The Dutch, under the energetic direction of de Witt, experienced little difficulty because of the big shipbuilding programme which had been put in hand after the first Anglo-Dutch War. They were able to man their fleet, too, because of the large reserve of seafaring men which they could draw on, and because of the comparatively (if only 'comparatively') good conditions which they could offer the men, in the light of the opportunities of making a living which they might find ashore.

In England, on the other hand, the fitting-out and manning of the fleet were, as usual, handicapped by the lack of money. Writing to Pepys from Chatham Dockyard on 12 October 1664, Peter Pett complained that not enough men were employed in the yard to enable necessary work to be done, and he estimated that he would need a thousand more to carry out the programme of repairing and fitting out ships. His later statement in the same letter, that of the oars delivered recently to the yard 'not one of eight is worth anything',[1] reveals the deficiencies in supply which so seriously hampered the equipping of the fleet.

As for manning the ships, the method of impressment had to be used to make up the crews, since volunteers were understandably hard to find. The quality of the pressed men was usually very poor, and many of them must have been a liability once they were afloat. On 1 December 1664 Peter Pett wrote to Pepys about pressed men who had been sent to Chatham to complete the

---

[1] C.S.P.D., 1664-5, p. 30.

crews of some of the ships there. He referred to them as 'those pitiful pressed creatures who are fit for nothing but to fill the ships full of vermin'; and a few days earlier in a previous letter to Pepys he had described the unfortunate victims in equally scathing terms as 'in no way fit for the service, being made up of all sorts of country trades, and such a ragged crew as never was seen'.[1]

Nevertheless, in spite of all the difficulties—and it says much for the harassed members of the Navy Board that the task was accomplished—by the time England formally declared war on the United Provinces, on 4 March 1665, a fleet of just over 100 vessels, including fireships,[2] had been made ready. The Duke of York, as commander-in-chief, flew his flag in the *Royal Charles* at the head of the red (centre) squadron; Prince Rupert was in command of the white (van); and Montagu, Earl of Sandwich, led the blue (rear) squadron.

The Dutch for their part had also assembled a fleet of over 100 vessels including fireships, and this was put under the command of Van Wassenaer van Obdam. Because of the rivalries among the various admiralties, and not primarily for any tactical reasons, the fleet was divided into no fewer than seven squadrons, and each of these was sub-divided into three smaller units. When the English and Dutch fleets met in the first major engagement of the war in Southwold Bay off Lowestoft on 3 June 1665, the division of the Dutch fleet was one of the causes of the defeat which it suffered, in which Obdam himself was lost with about 400 of his crew when his flagship, the *Eendracht*, blew up during a combat with the *Royal Charles*. After the loss of the commander-in-chief the Dutch fleet set sail for home, pursued by the victorious English. Then occurred a development which almost certainly saved the Dutch from further punishment, and which led afterwards to much recrimination in England.

The Duke of York, on board the *Royal Charles*, before retiring to his cabin for some sleep, gave orders that the pursuit of the retreating Dutch fleet should be continued throughout the night.

[1] C.S.P.D., 1664–5, p. 100, p. 92.
[2] These were vessels crammed with combustible material which were sent alongside enemy ships to set them on fire.

However, during his absence his gentleman-in-waiting, Henry Brouncker, brother of Lord Brouncker, went to Captain John Harman with an order to shorten sail. Since Brouncker affirmed that the fresh order had come from the Duke himself, Harman complied; the captains of the other ships followed suit, and the result was that when daylight broke the English fleet was too far behind to prevent the Dutch from escaping.

The Duke of York later denied that he had given any order to Brouncker that sail should be shortened; and to show his disapproval he dismissed Brouncker from his service. On 21 April 1668 the House of Commons met to discuss the incident, despite the fact that Brouncker, who was a member of the House and had been ordered to attend, was not present. After debate it was resolved that Brouncker should be expelled, that he was 'guilty of bringing pretended orders from his Royal Highness', and that he should be impeached for the misdemeanour.[1]

The Dutch had much greater cause than the English to be dissatisfied with the result of the battle, for they had suffered an inglorious reverse. Jan Evertsen, the Lieutenant-Admiral of the Zeeland squadron, and second-in-command to Obdam, was thrown into a river when he returned by the enraged citizens of Brielle, who sought thus to express their feelings that the fleet had been defeated through incompetence and cowardice. A commission of inquiry was later set up at The Hague to inquire into the causes of the defeat, and Evertsen was exonerated. A number of other officers were, however, found guilty of neglect of duty and cowardice, and some of these were shot, and others publicly degraded and dismissed the service.

After the Southwold Bay *débâcle* the Dutch laboured hard to restore their shattered fleet, and to such effect that within two months their ships were seaworthy again. This time the fleet was put under command of Cornelis Tromp, son of the great admiral who had perished in the first Anglo-Dutch War. In August 1665, however, de Ruyter arrived back from the West Indies, and at the prompting of de Witt and the States of Holland, Tromp—whom de Witt disliked and distrusted as an Orangist—was superseded

---

[1] *Journals of the House of Commons*, Vol. IX, 1667–87.

and his position as commander-in-chief given to de Ruyter. It says much for Tromp that he eventually agreed to serve under de Ruyter; but he never forgot or forgave the humiliation which he had been made to suffer, and for which he considered Johan de Witt responsible.

The Grand Pensionary himself took part in some fleet operations at this time, for he was one of three deputies appointed by the States-General to accompany a fleet in an operation which brought back safely to the United Provinces a number of merchant ships from the Mediterranean and the East Indies which had previously been unsuccessfully attacked by the English on 2 August 1665 while they were sheltering in Bergen harbour. After this rescue operation had been carried out by the Dutch there was a temporary lull in the war because of the onset of winter, which made major fleet operations impossible.

In January 1666 France and Denmark declared war on England, France because of her treaty with the Dutch made in 1662, and Denmark because of the English raid on Bergen, which at that time was Danish territory. Both in England and in the United Provinces great efforts were made to re-fit the fleets for the campaign of 1666, and each country managed to equip a force of about eighty vessels. De Ruyter remained in command of the Dutch fleet, and Prince Rupert and the Duke of Albemarle were appointed joint commanders of the English. After the Battle of Lowestoft Charles II had decided that for reasons of State the life of his brother, the Duke of York, ought not to be risked again in battle.

At the end of May the Government in London was led to believe that the French fleet intended to sail up the Channel in order to join with the Dutch. Prince Rupert was accordingly sent down Channel with a squadron of some twenty ships to try to intercept the French. Three days later, on 1 June 1666, Albemarle, with the remaining English ships, sailed northwards from the vicinity of the North Foreland, and at about midday he sighted the Dutch fleet which was riding at anchor some miles off Ostend. The English at once opened fire on the rear of the Dutch fleet, which was under command of Cornelis Tromp, and thus began what is known as the 'Four Days' Battle', one of the most fiercely fought and protracted fights ever to have taken place at sea.

De Ruyter, commanding the centre of the Dutch fleet, and Jan Evertsen, in command of the van, came to Tromp's aid, and a hard struggle followed, in which there were many dramatic episodes. The most notable of these, perhaps, was the death of Vice-Admiral Sir William Berkeley, who was flying his flag in the *Swiftsure*. His ship came under Dutch fire from all directions, was eventually cut off completely from the rest of the English fleet, and, in a badly disabled state, was boarded by the Dutch. Berkeley was shot in the throat, but even then refused to surrender, and retired mortally wounded to his cabin. There, when the Dutch followed him, they found him lying dead.

The fighting on the first day of the Four Days' Battle continued till 10 p.m., but then the English fleet, which had suffered considerable damage, stood to the westward. The next day, Saturday 2 June, the fighting was resumed about seven in the morning, and once again the English were badly mauled, and were forced to continue their withdrawal westwards. In the early morning of Sunday 3 June, the fleet was redeployed, so that disabled ships could be protected by a rearguard of sixteen of the largest men-of-war, which formed a shield between them and the pursuing Dutch.

At about 2 p.m. the Dutch had managed to advance to within cannon-shot, but at that moment the sails of another squadron were seen emerging from the south horizon. These ships, fortunately for the English, proved to be those under Prince Rupert's command which were returning from their foray down the Channel. Despite the reinforcement, however, the English retreat continued and during this phase of the battle the *Royal Prince*, a fine ship of ninety guns flying the flag of Admiral Sir George Ayscue, went aground on the Galloper Sands and was forced to yield to the Dutch, who set her on fire after they had taken off the surviving members of the crew.

At 8 a.m. on Monday 4 June, the two fleets made contact again, and another bout of fighting ensued. By now, both English and Dutch were exhausted, and the Dutch, who were far from base and were running short of gunpowder, disengaged and sailed for home. The English had suffered much more grievously than the Dutch in the fighting, and were in no shape to pursue them, so they too made for harbour. John Evelyn saw the ships a few days later, on 17 June 1666, when he visited Sheerness, and he noted in his diary:

Here I beheld that sad spectacle, namely more than halfe of that gallant bulwark of the Kingdome miserably shattered, hardly a vessell intire, but appearing rather so many wracks and hulls, so cruely had the Dutch mangled us.

Once again both sides worked feverishly to repair and refit their damaged ships, and by the end of July the fleets were able to put to sea again. On 25 July 1666 another action took place, off the North Foreland, and this battle, called the St. James's Day Fight, was a victory for the English, partly as a result of the impetuosity of Cornelis Tromp, who separated himself with his squadron from the main body of the Dutch fleet, and fought a subsidiary action of his own. After the battle de Ruyter complained to the States-General about Tromp's lack of fleet discipline, and as a result the States of Holland in August relieved Tromp of his commission until further orders.

Meanwhile the English took advantage of the temporary supremacy at sea which they had gained as a result of their victory on St. James' Day, and they carried out a damaging raid on a large number of Dutch merchant ships which were lying at anchor in the Vlie Channel off the island of Terschelling. On 8 August 1666 a squadron under Sir Robert Holmes was sent into the Vlie to capture or destroy these ships, and the operation, carried out in difficult waters, was facilitated by the help given by a Dutch traitor, Laurens Heemskerck. There were about 150 merchant vessels all told sheltering in the Vlie and, as they were guarded by only two Dutch men-of-war, Holmes's squadron found little opposition. On 9 August they sent in fireships against the merchantmen, and only a few of them managed to escape the general conflagration which followed, and which came to be called in England, with triumphant satisfaction, 'Holmes's Bonfire'. Not content with destroying the merchant ships, Holmes led a small force ashore on the island of Terschelling the next day, 10 August, and this destroyed storehouses and a large number of dwellings.

In England the exploit was celebrated as a notable victory. One contemporary broadsheet was entitled: *Joyfull News for England, or, a Congratulatory Verse upon our late happy Success in Firing 150 Dutch Ships in their own Harbours*, and the writer declared:

> The Startled States (again) shall never boast
> Of things nere done, bravad'ing on our Coast.
> No more Apostate Holland shall proclaim
> Those partiall conquests, which but brand her name.
> Now the Delusion's o'er, they plainly see,
> What once they were, what now they ought to be.
> Draw up your Sluces, ye may quench a flame,
> But never hope to wash away the Shame.[1]

The total loss to the Dutch resulting from Holmes's Bonfire ran into millions of guilders, but the resentment they felt over this was exceeded by the bitter feelings evoked by what the Dutch considered to be a wanton attack on poor people's dwellings. The Great Fire of London, which began a few weeks later on 2 September 1666, was widely regarded in the United Provinces as a divine punishment inflicted on the English for their iniquitous behaviour on Terschelling.

In September, shortly after the disaster, Johan de Witt, appointed by the States-General to be Commissioner with the fleet, went on board the flagship the *Zeven Provinciën*, and sail was set for the English coast, with the Grand Pensionary in fighting mood, and burning to avenge the recent humiliation by some retaliatory action on the English shore. However, de Ruyter, who was suffering from fever, had to be sent back home at the beginning of October; and a little while afterwards the fleet was recalled, without any attempt having been made at a landing.

Despite the victory of the Dutch in the Four Days' Battle, the campaign of 1666 had on the whole been unsatisfactory for the United Provinces. The English had fared somewhat better, and this must partly be ascribed to the fact that in November 1665

[1] British Museum, Luttrell Collection, *Proclamations and Broadsides*, Vol. III, No. 95.

Parliament had voted an additional sum of £1,250,000 for carrying on the war. This money took time to come into the exchequer, however, and the naval administration continued to be harassed by lack of funds. As a result the morale of the seamen and dockyardmen remained low, because of the conditions which they were forced to endure.

In October 1664 John Evelyn had been appointed one of the Commissioners for the care of the sick and wounded, and on more than one occasion he expressed in writing his sympathy for his unfortunate charges, whom he was unable to succour as he would have wished, through lack of proper provision. Thus on 3 October 1665 he wrote to Pepys from his house at Sayes Court, Deptford, that it was impossible for him to find accommodation for all the sick and wounded men who were being continually put ashore. These unfortunates, Evelyn said, went despairingly from one place to another, and often perished on the way. There was no more accommodation for them in Chatham and Gravesend, and so all the villages around were 'peopled with the poor miserable creatures'.[1]

On 7 October Pepys recorded in his diary:

Did business, though not much, at the office; because of the horrible crowd and lamentable moan of the poor seamen that lie starving in the streets for lack of money. Which do trouble and perplex me to the heart; and more at noon when we were to go through them, for then above a whole hundred of them followed us, some cursing, some swearing, and some praying to us.

The next day he wrote: 'I think of twenty-two ships we shall make shift to get out seven (God help us!), men being sick, or provisions lacking.' On the same theme, the troubles caused by lack of funds, Pepys remarked again, sadly, on 31 October: 'Want of money in the Navy puts everything out of order; men grow mutinous.'

Just over a week later, on 7 November, Lord Brouncker sent to Pepys an account of the sufferings of the seamen at Chatham which he had received from Peter Pett. In this Pett spoke of the

[1] C.S.P.D., 1665–6, p. 3.

'sad conditions' at Chatham, caused by 'the multitude of sick and
wounded sent from the fleet', also by the arrival of seamen from
all parts of the country to join their ships at Chatham. These men
had been given so small an allowance for their journey, even if
they had to travel from places far away, that they were 'obliged to
sell their rags to keep themselves from starving'.[1]

The men rebelled against such treatment, and desperate action
against impressment was not uncommon. Thus in December 1666
a gang of forty seamen armed with pistols and swords forced open
the door of a building in Dartford where impressed men had
been left in the charge of the local constable, and they released the
imprisoned men.[2] The wives of the seamen, in their despair, also
did what they could from time to time to call attention to their
grievances, and in his diary on 10 July 1666 Pepys recalled such an
occasion:

To the office; the yard being very full of women (I believe above three
hundred) coming to get money for their husbands and friends that are
prisoners in Holland; and they lay clamouring and swearing and cursing us, that my wife and I were afraid to send a venison-pasty that we
have for supper tonight to the cook's to be baked, for fear of their
offering violence to it. . . .

On 21 July Pepys recorded that he had had a discussion with
Peter Pett, who had come up to London to see him, and that Pett
had told him 'how infinite are the disorders among the commanders and all officers of the fleet. No discipline, nothing but
cursing and swearing, and everybody doing what they please.'

The conditions in the dockyards were as bad as those in the
fleet. Because of lack of money there was lack of stores; because of
lack of stores there was lack of employment for the dockyardmen;
and above all, because of lack of money there was no pay. This in
turn caused wholesale theft and frequent disorders, as well as a
multitude of corrupt practices of which Chatham Dockyard provided many examples. In April 1665 Sir John Mennes, writing
from there to Pepys, had referred to the great number of men
in the yard who were unemployed; he added that they were

[1] Ibid., p. 45.   [2] C.S.P.D., 1666-7, p. 334.

clamorous for their money, since they had not been paid for nine months.[1]

The men had to be retained on the books till they were paid, and as they could not be paid, spent their days in idleness, or were employed in uneconomic manner. Thus Pepys recorded on 2 October 1665 how he visited Chatham Dockyard, in company with Commissioner Pett, who walked around with him:

Among other things a team of four horses came close by us, he [Pett] being with me, drawing a piece of timber that I am confident one man could easily have carried upon his back. I made the horses be taken away, and a man or two to take the timber away with their hands.

Just over a month later, on 4 November 1665, about 300 workmen in the yard, caulkers and carpenters, mutinied because some of their work had been taken away from them; and on 26 January 1666 Commissioner Peter Pett wrote to Pepys to say that he was finding it difficult to persuade the skilled men, the shipwrights, to continue at work because of the arrears of pay due to them.[2] In a letter from Sir John Mennes to the Navy Board, written from Chatham on 11 August 1666, he estimated that £18,000 was owing in wages to the men of the yard, and he said that they were cutting up good government timber which their wives and children came into the yard to collect, in order later to sell it.

Pepys attended a meeting in Whitehall on 7 October 1666 which was attended by the King, the Duke of York, Prince Rupert, Clarendon, the Duke of Albemarle, and the members of the Navy Board. Pepys spoke, 'laying open', as he related in his diary: 'the ill state of the navy; by the greatness of the debt; greatness of the work to do against next year; the time and materials it would take, and our incapacity, through a total want of money'. Pepys thought, so he said, that he had made a good speech; but the first reaction was an angry reply from Prince Rupert, who thought that aspersions had been cast upon him. Pepys judged it expedient to express his regret that Prince Rupert had taken offence, but he sturdily affirmed that what he had said was, in effect, a summary of an account received from certain

[1] C.S.P.D., 1664–5, p. 304.   [2] C.S.P.D., 1665–6, p. 219.

officers of the fleet who had been asked to make a report to the
Navy Board. After this, Pepys related in his diary, there was 'a
long silence on all hands', during which nobody supported the
Prince, or attempted to refute what Pepys had said; and finally
Pepys and the other members of the Navy Board withdrew.

Later, 'after all this pains', in Pepys' words, the King undertook
to advance £5,000 to £6,000 for naval needs, though the members of the Navy Board had mentioned a sum of £50,000 as being
immediately necessary. It is hardly surprising therefore to find
Pepys writing despondently in his diary on 19 October 1666 that
there was 'nothing but distraction and confusion in the affairs of
the Navy'.

Meanwhile the morale of the Government and the people had
been affected by two great calamities—the Great Plague of 1665
during which nearly 70,000 people died in London alone, and
which spread to other parts of the country in 1666, and the Great
Fire of London which occurred in September of that year. The
fire, which in four days destroyed 13,000 buildings, badly affected
the City, which was an important source of Government loans;
but in addition to the material loss the fire had a lowering effect on
people's morale. In a superstitious age, it was widely construed as
a sign that God was temporarily not with the English, and, indeed,
was punishing them for their sins.

In such circumstances, therefore, it is not surprising that in the
autumn of 1666 there was despondency in Whitehall, and a disposition for peace. In October Parliament did indeed vote a
further £1,800,000 for the prosecution of the war, but the Bill
was not passed till January 1667, so that nothing could be done
immediately to alleviate the financial stringency from which the
navy was suffering. Moreover, owing to the time-lag between
the allocation of a parliamentary grant and the actual receipt of the
money by the Crown, no appreciable financial respite was to be
expected for months. Because of all these circumstances—war-
weariness aggravated by the effects of the plague and fire, and
above all because of the lack of ready money—Charles was ready
at the end of 1666 to consider negotiations for peace.

The Dutch, for their part, were equally willing. They were

suffering huge losses through the interruption of their seaborne commerce, and the hindrance of their herring fishery in the North Sea. Moreover, since in contrast to the English they had lavished large sums on the furtherance of the war, taxation had greatly increased, and this bore heavily on the rich burghers who controlled policy. In addition the Dutch were suspicious of designs which they thought their nominal ally, Louis XIV of France, had on the Spanish Netherlands, which lay on the southern border of the United Provinces.

Already in July 1666 a Swedish offer to mediate had been accepted by both the English and Dutch, but meanwhile Charles II, sensing that the Dutch would not be prepared to make peace at any price, entered into secret negotiations with Louis XIV in the hope that the French king would undertake to bring pressure on the Dutch to make peace. At the same time Charles opened another secret line of negotiation, this time with the Dutch, through the envoy of the Holy Roman Emperor, Lisola. Even during the war contacts between London and The Hague had not ceased altogether, and after the Four Days' Battle in June 1666 the Dutch, from respect for the bravery of Sir William Berkeley, had had his body embalmed and placed in the Grote Kerk in The Hague. They then sent a message to Charles II offering to send Berkeley's body back to England for burial. Charles thanked the States-General, accepted the offer, and gave the Dutch vessel which brought back Berkeley's body a safe-conduct.

This round of civilities helped to create a more favourable atmosphere between the two countries, and discussions with the Dutch progressed so far that by the end of January 1667 the stage had been reached of deciding where an eventual peace conference should be held. Charles suggested The Hague, but de Witt objected to this because it was a notoriously Orangist town. Meanwhile the Earl of St. Albans, who had been conducting the secret negotiations with Louis XIV, led Charles to believe that provided certain French stipulations were met, Louis would bring pressure to bear on the Dutch to induce them to make peace. This seemed an attractive proposition, since the feelers which Lisola had put out to the Dutch had revealed that de Witt was not ready to make peace on the terms which Charles had in mind.

At the centre of this tangled web of diplomatic negotiations sat Henry Bennet, Earl of Arlington, the more important of the two Secretaries of State who were responsible for foreign relations. In April 1666 Arlington had married a Dutch woman, Isabella, daughter of Louis of Nassau, Lord of Beverwaert, who was an illegitimate son of Prince Maurice of Nassau. The marriage was financially advantageous to Arlington, for his bride brought with her a large dowry amounting to 100,000 guilders. Politically it seems to have occasioned no comment at all, and indeed, despite the fact that England and the United Provinces were at war, Arlington's Dutch bride was appointed a lady of the bedchamber to the Queen of England.

After much discussion it was finally agreed, on 18 March, that peace negotiations should take place at Breda, but before this Charles and his advisers had already taken a decision which was to have momentous consequences. Faced with the impossibility of fitting out a fleet for the approaching campaigning season, because of lack of funds, and relying on Louis XIV to coerce or cajole the Dutch into accepting peace terms acceptable to England, they gambled on the chance that pending the outcome of the negotiations the Dutch would observe an unofficial truce.

A decision was therefore taken not to fit out the customary large battle fleet for 1667, but instead to maintain one or two small squadrons based on widely separated ports, to defend English and harass Dutch merchant shipping. Meanwhile, in default of the protection afforded by a battle fleet, it was also decided that various measures should be taken to defend ports and dockyards from possible enemy attacks. In his diary for 6 March 1667 Pepys related:

To Whitehall; and here the Duke of York did acquaint us (and the King did the like also afterwards coming in) with his resolution of altering the manner of the war this year: that is, we shall keep what fleet we have abroad in several squadrons. So that now all is come out . . .

On 1 April Pepys took a walk in Whitehall with Sir William Coventry, and they talked, inevitably, of the state of the Navy and the possibility of peace. Coventry conceded that England must have a peace, since no fleet could be fitted out. But, said Pepys, 'to use his own words, he feels that we shall soon have enough of fighting in this new way that we have thought on for this year'.

In just over two months from then events were to occur which proved that Sir William Coventry's fears were fully justified. These events were, however, to exceed in calamity for England anything which Coventry could possibly have had in mind when talking to Pepys on that April morning in the garden of the Royal Palace of Whitehall.

CHAPTER V

The Best Plenipotentiary for Peace

ALREADY IN THE reign of Charles I Sir William Monson, in his tract entitled: *A Project for the Safety of his Majesty's Navy; and the convenience and Inconvenience in keeping it at Chatham or Portsmouth* had considered the possibility of a Dutch attack on the Medway. After recommending that the entire fleet should be kept in the river, he continued:

And yet I must confess, they [i.e. the ships] are not altogether so safe and secure from the assault of a fleet that shall be brought with an easterly wind; and therefore it behoves us to be cautious and wary of it, as follows. . . . Somewhat I will say in particular of the state of our Navy at Chatham, and the danger that may befall us from Holland, if they become enemies to us, as also shew the way of prevention. Holland, by reason of their abundance of shipping, the number of soldiers quartered in all parts of their country, and their daily and speedy use in gathering their forces together for present service, will give us the less suspicion if they should intend any sudden stratagem upon us. And the first thing that they will attend is the opportunity of a settled easterly wind, to bring their ships without striking sail as high as Gravesend, and there suddenly, without resistance, put eight or ten thousand men on the Kentish shore to march to Upnor Castle not above four or five miles from thence, which castle all men know is able to make no resistance, the castle being both weak and weakly provided. Suppose they possessing it, and directing their ships at Gravesend to repair thither, they have his Majesty's navy at their mercy, which is a thing it fears me to think on. . . .

Monson, having pointed out the danger, suggested various preventive measures:

For prevention thereof it were fit and convenient that Upnor Castle be strongly and sufficiently fortified, as well to the landward as to the river, that it may be out of the power of an enemy suddenly to sur-

prise it ... And so much as concerns the defence of the river, by boom-
ing, and making sconces upon it, I say sufficiently in my stratagems;
but seeing this is a matter of so great import as the safety of our navy,
I advise and wish, in case our ships shall be assailed, that the ordnance,
or greatest part of them, be kept continually aboard the ships, both
mounted and fitted. The powder and shot to be likewise kept continually on board....[1]

Monson's extraordinary prescience was in vain; for not only
were the defences of the Medway not improved, but they were
allowed slowly to deteriorate. The chain placed across the river at
Upnor in 1585 had later been replaced by a boom defence of
floating timber, but this again had been dispensed with in the
reign of Charles I. During the Protectorate, in 1658, there was a
plan to place another boom across the river, probably at Upnor,
but there is no record that this was ever done.

Fortifications along the shores of the Medway were similarly
neglected. In 1660 Upnor Castle's garrison comprised a mere
twenty to thirty men; and in November 1666 the garrison was
actually paid off and the castle taken over by ordnance officers for
storage purposes. Just below Upnor Castle two slight fortifications called Bay and Warham Sconces had been constructed at the
beginning of the seventeenth century to add to the defence provided by Upnor Castle itself. In the reign of James I the founda-
tions of the gun platform in Warham Sconce were reported to
have been washed away, and it seems that these two small fortifications were subsequently allowed to fall into ruin. Thus, below
Upnor Castle, right to the mouth of the Medway, there was no
other fortification, and it was only very tardily that steps were
taken to remedy this serious deficiency.

In August 1665 ground was surveyed for a dockyard at Sheerness, and to protect the yard and the Medway it was later, in
December 1666, decided to construct a fort on the north-western
point of the Isle of Sheppey, at Sheerness. In his diary on 27
February 1667 Pepys recorded that Charles II and the Duke of
York had gone down to Sheerness 'to lay out the design' of the
fort; and on 20 March 1667 Sir William Penn, Sir Edward

[1] M. Oppenheim (ed.), *The Naval Tracts of Sir William Monson*, Navy Records Society,
Vol. V, pp. 12–14.

Spragge, Peter Pett, Phineas Pett, and twelve other officials held a consultation at Sheerness and decided that the gun 'platform' or emplacement should be built at Sheerness Point.

The subsequent history of the project is a sad tale of delay and inadequacy. A committee of the House of Commons which was appointed in 1668 to inquire into the miscarriages of the war found that from 27 April 1667, when Captain Valentine Price was sent to Sheerness by the Ordnance Commissioners to superintend the construction of the fort, the work was carried on in a dilatory way because of the lack of workmen; seldom more than ten men were employed at any one time. The difficulty of finding men ready to work at Sheerness arose not only from the usual lack of ready money, which made the payment of their wages unreliable, but also from the bad conditions: there was a lack of proper facilities for the supply of such necessities as food and water. As a result the labour force was small, the men appear to have been pressed, and so to have worked perfunctorily, so that the fort was still unfinished in June 1667.

At some time early in 1667 a decision was taken to place a chain across the river once more as a reinforcement of its defences; but again unconscionable delays occurred in getting the chain made and installed. On 23 March Pepys referred to the chain in his diary entry for that day:

At the office, where Sir William Pen came, being returned from Chatham, from considering the means of fortifying the River Medway, by a chain at the stakes, and ships laid there with guns to keep the enemy from coming up to burn our ships; all our care being now to fortify ourselves against their invading us.

On 27 April 1667 Peter Pett informed the Navy Board that Mr. Ruffhead, who was making the chain, had promised that it would be ready in a few days' time. It would have been ready sooner, Pett thought fit to add, if Ruffhead had been paid some money meanwhile on account.[1] Peter Pett wrote again to the Navy Board on 10 May, informing them that the chain was due to arrive at Chatham the following day; and he stated that all necessary preparations had been completed for installing it. Another

[1] C.S.P.D., 1667, pp. 57–8.

week passed, however, before he was able to write, on 18 May, that the chain had been 'hove over from side to side' of the river that afternoon.

In another letter Pett said that the position of the chain was 'a little beyond Gillingham';[1] and from other evidence it is clear that it must have stretched across the Medway from a point a little down-river from Gillingham to an opposite point on Hoo Salt Marsh. In the seventeenth century the Medway was narrower in this part of Gillingham Reach than it is today, and the saltings lying off-shore were much more extensive, so that the end of the chain on the Gillingham side of the river may have been fixed on one of these saltings. Today the width of the river at low water in Gillingham Reach is some 500 yards, so that even if the chain ended on one of the saltings and not on the river bank at Gillingham, it must have been of considerable length. Pepys inspected the chain during one of his visits to Chatham and had one of its links measured. He said that it was found to be $6\frac{1}{4}$ inches 'in circumference', but it is unlikely that he meant by this that the overall length of each link was of this dimension, for this would mean that a link would have measured only about $2\frac{1}{2}$ inches long by $1\frac{1}{2}$ inches wide. Such a size of link would hardly have been sufficient to make a chain strong enough to bar the way to large ships. It is much more likely that by 'circumference' Pepys meant the thickness of each link. If this is so, a circumference of $6\frac{1}{4}$ inches would result in a chain with links 2 inches thick. Each link would therefore be proportionately massive in size, and the total weight of the chain was, in fact, nearly $14\frac{1}{2}$ tons, according to a survey made in May 1667.[2]

This was an enormous weight, and to prevent the chain from sinking too deep in the water it was supported by four large floating stages evenly spaced across the Medway. Even so, between the floats the chain sank to a depth of nearly 9 feet under the surface, because of its weight. At each end of the chain there were windlasses to haul it as taut as possible, and as these had to be operated by manual labour, the difficulty in keeping the chain near to the surface of the water must have been great.

[1] State Papers, (S.P.) 46 (136), f. 488.   [2] C.S.P.D., Addenda, 1660–85, p. 187.

The chain itself was not considered strong enough to resist a determined effort to break it, and so it was strengthened with cables taken from the man-of-war, the *Monmouth*. According to some contemporary Dutch accounts masts had also been driven into the river bed and cables slung between these as an additional reinforcement of the chain, and this is confirmed by a letter dated 2 September 1667 written by the Masters of Attendance[1] at Chatham to the Navy Board.

Instructions for safeguarding the chain by stationing two ships near it were included in a directive for strengthening the defences of the Medway sent by the Duke of York to the Navy Board on 25 March 1667. He wrote:

Gentlemen,
Having lately directed that the safety of his Majesty's ships in the river of Medway should be taken into consideration upon the place, by some persons sent down to that purpose, upon the report which they have since made I desire you to give order that the *Unity* may have 20 seamen added to the 40 already allowed, and that, besides the *Dolphin* fireship already about Sheerness, one other of the first ready (except those appointed for the West Indies) may be sent thither, and two other to lie within the Chain at Chatham [*sic*] to be ready for any occasion; that the *Unity*, *Dolphin* fireship and the two ketches now attending there may be forthwith cleaned; that each ship and the ketches may have sheer-hooks, grapnels and chains furnished them, with each a good pinnace with ten oars, with a small grapnel and chain. This is what I have at present to direct you for Sheerness.

As for the upper part of the River of Medway, I desire you to take care that all his Majesty's ships may be moored in the safest places you can, especially the first and second-rate ships, and that, besides the completing the chain for their further security, the ships *Charles V* and *Matthias*[2] may be moored within the chain, in such manner as that upon occasion they may bring their broadsides to bear upon the chain; and that a competent number of seamen may be allowed to be borne on them; that 30 good pinnaces, well fitted with oars, grapnels and chains may be provided in readiness. . . .[3]

---

[1] These were senior dockyard officials who were responsible for moving and fitting out ships.

[2] Both these ships had been captured from the Dutch, the former at the Battle of Lowestoft in 1665, the latter in 1653 during the first Anglo-Dutch War.

[3] C.S.P.D., 1666–7, p. xxxi.

As usual, the defence preparations in the Medway went forward very slowly, because of the lack of money and the consequent difficulty in procuring stores and paying the dockyardmen and seamen. On 27 April, for example, Peter Pett wrote to the Navy Board to say that if money was not forthcoming to settle outstanding bills, 'it will be impossible to answer the expectations of His Majesty and His Royal Highness [i.e. the Duke of York] there being so little provision in store'.[1] On 15 May Pett wrote again to the Navy Board about conditions in the dockyard at Chatham. The 'sad cries' of the dockyardmen for want of their money were so great, said Pett, that he was obliged to ask the members of the Board to do all they could to procure some money in order that the men could be paid. He went on to say that there was a great lack of timber in the dockyard, and declared that if supplies were not sent soon he would be forced to discharge many of the workmen. He enclosed with his letter a petition signed by the shipwrights and workmen in the yard. In this they asked Pett to try to get their wages paid to them without delay, because otherwise they, with their wives and children, would perish, since nobody would give them credit and so they could get no food. They reminded Pett, in conclusion, that their wages were more than twelve months in arrear.[2]

Pett must have been informed that no money was available to pay the men, for on 1 May 1667 he wrote again to the Navy Board, saying he was sorry to hear that there was so little hope of money 'for satisfying poor people whose cries are great'.[3] On 18 May he wrote to say that the pinnaces which the Duke of York had ordered had almost all been built, but that oars were lacking for them. He once again emphasized that there was no plank in store, and added that none had been supplied for a long time.[4] The question of the oars was taken up again, as late as 5 June 1667, by Sir William Coventry, in a letter to the Navy Board. By this time a supply of oars had been procured from Harwich; but, said Coventry, these had been found 'crooked and unserviceable'.[5]

[1] C.S.P.D., 1667, pp. 57–8.   [2] Ibid., 1667, p. 101.
[3] C.S.P.D., Addenda, 1660–85, p. 180.   [4] Ibid., p. 185.
[5] Ibid., p. 187.

Apart from the difficulty of obtaining indispensable stores, work in the dockyard at Chatham suffered from the insubordination of the men, which was primarily due to the failure of the Government to pay them their wages. Their disregard for authority was reflected, for example, in general and prolonged absenteeism. Edward Gregory, Clerk of the Check at Chatham, wrote to the Navy Board on 7 June 1667 referring specifically to this abuse, and he asked helplessly for advice as to how he should keep the men to their duty.

The seamen too were in no better shape. On 21 December 1666 a correspondent of Joseph Williamson, secretary to Lord Arlington, said that many sailors had deserted from the Royal Navy in order to serve in merchant ships. The sailors alleged, so the correspondent said, that they were forced to give naval paymasters and their clerks half the pay due to them, in order to get the other half. Soldiers who were sent to reinforce the crews of some of the ships were of poor calibre, and in pitiful condition. On 11 March 1667, for example, Captain Thomas Trafford, of the *Unity* frigate lying as guardship off Sheerness, informed the Navy Board that soldiers who had been sent to his ship were thin and poorly clad, many of them were sick, and hardly one of them was worth his keep, since they were all 'poor silly lads and raw country fellows'.[1]

In the spring of 1667 the state of the fleet, and the general preparations in England for defence against a possible enemy attack, could hardly have been worse. On the other side of the North Sea, however, in the United Provinces, the situation was quite different. Johan de Witt was determined not to allow any talk of peace negotiations to deter him from his major purpose, which was to maintain a powerful fleet in being, no matter what the cost. This was to be a safeguard in case the peace negotiations with England failed but also more positively, to be used as a decisive weapon at the appropriate time. In December 1666 de Witt persuaded the States-General to approve the measures necessary for strengthening and fitting out a strong fleet, even though this meant an increase in taxation to cover the cost of 12 to 16 million guilders which was involved. As a result of the

[1] C.S.P.D., 1666–7, p. 557.

lavish expenditure a fine fleet comprising seventy-two men-of-war, twelve frigates, twenty-four fireships, and a number of small ancillary vessels such as armed yachts was soon being fitted out.

All through the early months of 1667 the Dutch shipyards and dockyards had been busy getting the ships ready for sea, and news of this activity soon reached Whitehall. On 1 February 1667 Samuel Tucker, writing from Rotterdam to Lord Arlington, said: 'The ice being now out of the waters here, men are set at work upon the Estates' shipps to fit them for service againe in the summer, and all endeavours are used herein.'[1] On 8 March Tucker wrote:

The Estates preparations for warr goes on with might and maine, and noe tyme is neglected in equiping the shipps, noe not soe much as Sundays, in soe much that the ffleet will be out very tymely this yeare. . . . Som will have it best to make peace with the sword in the hand.[2]

On 19 March 1667 the States-General appointed de Ruyter commander-in-chief of the fleet, and subsequently the other superior officers were nominated. These were admirals Aert Jansz. van Nes, Adriaen Banckert, Willem Joseph van Ghent, Jan Cornelisz. Meppel, and Hans Willem van Aylua. In April de Ruyter was busy supervising the preparations for getting the fleet ready for sea, but so far no plan of campaign had been officially communicated to the officers of the fleet.

Johan de Witt, a man predisposed by nature to favour bold courses, had always, from the very beginning of the war, considered the possibility of an armed raid on some part of the English coast, and such a project became even dearer to him after 1666 as a means of retaliation for Holmes's attack on Terschelling. Even before this, however, at the end of June 1666, the Dutch had contemplated a landing in some force. This was to reinforce a rebellion against the régime of Charles II which an English renegade, one Samuel Raven, had assured them could easily be started if he were landed and thus enabled to contact friends who would organize a rising. Raven's expectations proved to be quite without

[1] S.P. 84 (182) f. 19.   [2] Ibid., f. 65.

foundation, and the Dutch abandoned their scheme. Nevertheless de Witt kept constantly in mind the advantage which would accrue to the United Provinces from the successful carrying out of some such raid. He kept his thoughts on the subject very close to himself, and told only a few of his closest friends and advisers; and meanwhile he saw to it that the fleet preparations were carried vigorously forward. The fleet, he said, was to be the best plenipotentiary for peace.

Meanwhile on 14 May 1667 the English envoys entered Breda for the conference which, it was hoped in England, would bring peace. Negotiations began on 25 May, and awkward questions of precedence at once arose. These were solved by arranging that the conference chamber should have several doors, so that one ambassador would not be forced to follow another when he entered. Similarly, to avoid disputes about who should sit at the head of the table, a large round table was provided. Despite these subtle compromises, however, it soon became apparent that negotiations would be difficult, for the English envoys had instructions which reflected the belief of Charles II that the Dutch would be forced to make peace by their French ally, in accordance with the understanding reached between Charles and Louis XIV.

But the English king's assumption was wrong, and even while the Breda discussions were proceeding, de Witt was supervising the final preparations for the daring project which he had conceived, which was to effect a raid in the Thames and Medway, with a view to landing a considerable force to destroy dockyard installations and capture or destroy as many as possible of the English men-of-war which, as he knew from his intelligence sources, were laid up in the Medway.

Both the Thames and Medway are difficult rivers to navigate, the first because of the many sandbanks in the estuary, the second because of its twisting course and mudflats. De Witt therefore needed some Englishmen with a special knowledge of the two rivers, who would be willing to serve with the Dutch. He had no difficulty in finding such men. At his request the States-General ordered inquiries to be made in the prisons where captured English seamen were held, to discover whether among them there were any good pilots who were familiar with the navigation of the Thames and Medway. These men were to be asked whether they would take service with the Dutch in return for a 'commensurate reward'. It is not known what the response to the inquiry was; but as the conditions of the prisoners-of-war were very bad,[1] it is more than likely that a good number of volunteers were forthcoming, especially since subsequent reports from English sources refer to English seamen serving on board the Dutch ships.

The most notorious of the English who volunteered was one Robert Holland, of Boston in Lincolnshire. He was said to have served as a captain in the Navy during the Commonwealth, but to have resented the fact that thereafter no promotion came his way. For that reason he turned traitor and offered his services to the Dutch.[2] One of Lord Arlington's informants in the United Provinces, named Pierre du Moulin,[3] wrote a letter to Arlington, probably on 1 June 1667, in which he described a meeting with two renegade Englishmen, one of whom may well have been Holland. Du Moulin wrote:

Going to ye Texell, I happened to meet wth two Englishmen, who were going to de Ruyter and who, being then much in drink, did bragg before severall of us of ye letters they had for de Ruyter and ye great respect they should have both from ye Admirall and from ye whole fleet. Having no opportunity that night of speaking to them in private, I took an occasion the next day to enter into severall discourse wth them, and found ye one was halfe a fift monarchy man[4] whose ship was seized in ye Isle of Wight about a year before ye warr for some treasonable speeches against his Maj[ty]. . . . Ye other not so great a fanatick, but never the lesse a passionate fellow, who, as farr as I could gather from his discourse, hath lost his ship or goods for stealing ye King's customes. Amongst other things, that w[ch] I took most notice

[1] On 9 June, when some English prisoners were repatriated from Rotterdam, it was stated that they spoke much of the hard usage they had received, some of them not having seen the sun during the whole year when they were in prison (C.S.P.D., 1667, p. 164).

[2] Rawlinson MS. D.924, f. 232.

[3] Du Moulin was a French Huguenot who became a naturalized English subject in May 1664. He gained Arlington's favour, and was attached to various diplomatic missions. He later incurred Arlington's displeasure, fled to the United Provinces in 1672, and entered the service of the Prince of Orange. His activities are described by K. H. D. Haley in *William of Orange and the English Opposition 1672–4*, Oxford, 1953.

[4] One of the fanatical religious sects which sprang up in England during the seventeenth century.

of, is that they did inveigh very bitterly against ye burning, both of ye ships in ye Vlie and ye houses in ye Schelling, saying ye Dutch might easily be revenged of it and do ye like in England. I told them I did not think it so easy, and yt [that] in my opinion his Ma^{ty} had no consider-able port where he might feare any such attempt; to which they re-plyed yt I was mistaken, and yt to their knowledge it was no hard matter to enter into severall English ports and burn and destroy all ye ships there in spight of either blockhouses or forts . . . I found by all w^t they said, that they were fully resolved to serve ye Dutch to ye utmost of their power, and to that end were recommended from very good hands to de Ruyter.[1]

On 21 May 1667 Johan de Witt had written to Job de Wildt, secretary of the States-General, informing him that he intended to come to Texel to supervise the fitting out of the fleet, and to give final orders to de Ruyter. He said, however, that he wished first to speak with captains of vessels who had recently brought back Dutch prisoners-of-war from England (there had been prisoner-of-war exchanges since 1666), also with other persons who had recently come from England, in order to get full details of the strength and position of the English naval forces at Chatham and other places. De Witt concluded by asking de Wildt to seek out the skippers and other persons, and to make sure that they were available for discussions when he should arrive.[2] It is very likely that during this visit he spoke with Holland and other English renegades, and that he decided to recommend them to de Ruyter as pilots to be taken on the expedition.

Johan de Witt himself would undoubtedly have taken part in the operation which he had planned, but for the fact that his presence was considered indispensable at home, because of the peace negotiations at Breda. In May, however, he persuaded the States-General to appoint his elder brother Cornelis, Burgomaster of Dordrecht, as plenipotentiary of the States-General with the fleet. Cornelis was experienced in naval affairs—he had been a member of the Admiralty of the Maas for four years—and he was intelligent, brave, and resourceful. Even so, he was outshone by his brilliant brother, and though the elder, was very much under

[1] S.P. 84 (182), f. 131.
[2] R. Fruin and N. Japikse, *Brieven van Johan de Witt*, Amsterdam, 1912, Vol. III, 1665–9, p. 295.

Johan's domination. In getting him chosen as the States-General's plenipotentiary Johan ensured that he would be able to exercise the control which he wished, even though he was not present with the fleet. This was, in fact, to be effected by a continuous exchange of letters between the two brothers, after the fleet had set sail.

In these letters Johan counselled, exhorted, commended, and sometimes chided Cornelis, while the latter in his replies clearly showed that he accepted without question his younger brother's role of mentor. Cornelis arrived at Texel on 25 May, and later he went on board de Ruyter's flagship the *Zeven Provinciën*. The relationship between the two men, the plenipotentiary with ultimate authority deriving from the States-General, and the admiral, responsible for the actual conduct of operations, was very delicate, and could easily have led to divided counsels, friction, and disaster. But as it happened, Cornelis de Witt and de Ruyter liked and respected each other, and their association was to prove wholly successful. A good deal of the praise for this must be given to de Ruyter, who showed once again what a truly great leader he was by accommodating himself to this sea-partnership.

One of Johan de Witt's major preoccupations throughout the spring of 1667 had been to keep his enterprise secret from all but two or three of his most trusted intimates, and he was also concerned about the depredations which English and Scots privateers had been making on Dutch shipping in the North Sea. In order both to try to put a stop to these and also to divert attention from the concentration of the fleet in the Dutch harbours, he dispatched van Ghent in April 1667 with a small force of some twenty ships to the Firth of Forth. The squadron entered the firth at the end of April, but caused little damage and captured only a few small vessels. It did, however, help to divert attention in England from the preparation of the main fleet, which by the end of May was almost complete.

A large contingent of troops, numbering between 3,000 and 4,000, had been assembled for embarkation, and there were also detachments of the newly formed sea-soldiers or marines. Remarkably, it was an Englishman named Thomas Dolman, who had the rank of colonel, who was put in command of these troops. Dolman is a fascinating but shadowy figure about whom very little is known, despite his closeness to the brothers de Witt and the importance which the Dutch clearly attached to his services. The English and Scots regiments which had fought for the Dutch since the reign of Elizabeth had been disbanded when the first Anglo-Dutch war broke out in 1652, but after the war had ended some new regiments were formed, and Dolman had been appointed commander of one of these by a resolution of the States of Holland in March 1665, shortly after the outbreak of the second Anglo-Dutch war. According to Edmund Ludlow Dolman was 'an experienc'd officer . . . who for not rendring himself within the time limited by the late proclamation, had incurred the penalty of treason by virtue of a late act passed at Westminster'.[1] Ludlow was referring to an Act of Parliament passed in 1665 under which Dolman and a Thomas Scot and Joseph Bamfield were to be deemed guilty of treason if they did not surrender themselves by an appointed day. They failed to do so, and a proclamation attainting Dolman and a number of others was issued on 21 April 1666. From the available evidence therefore it seems that Dolman had incurred suspicion by his connection with the Dutch; and it is probable that he had fled to the United Provinces and offered his services to the Dutch because he refused to accept the Restoration. Whatever the reason for his coming to the United Provinces, he soon established himself with Johan de Witt, and the latter referred to him as a very intimate friend of Cornelis, and a faithful servant of the United Provinces.[2]

On 17 May de Ruyter had sailed with the Maas squadron for Texel, which had been appointed as the fleet rendezvous, and here he anchored on 25 May, and waited for the contingents of Zeeland and Friesland, which were delayed for various reasons. Van Ghent had joined him with the squadron which had been sent to the Firth of Forth, and while the fleet waited near Den Helder the States-General, in secret conclave, was deciding on the general strategy to be followed by the fleet. On 20 May the assembly had

[1] C. H. Firth (ed.), *The Memoirs of Edmund Ludlow, 1625–72*, Oxford, 1894, Vol. II, p. 400.
[2] R. Fruin and N. Japikse, *Brieven van Johan de Witt*, Amsterdam, 1912, Vol. III, 1665–9, p. 298.

passed a secret resolution instructing their plenipotentiary, Cornelis de Witt, to attempt a foray against the English coast at some point, and he was directed to take risks in the venture rather than return home without having attempted something.

By 27 May the Friesland and Zeeland ships had still not appeared, so shortly afterwards de Ruyter set sail with the vessels furnished by the other admiralties. Deputies of the States-General including Johan de Witt himself were present on board the *Zeven Provinciën* as the fleet left Texel and put to sea. Soon, however, they had to say farewell and to return ashore; but before doing so they handed to Cornelis de Witt the detailed instructions of the States-General for the operation. After the deputies had left Cornelis read out to de Ruyter and the other senior commanders the instructions which he had been given. These were that the fleet should first sail southwards along the coast to the Maas, where troops and stores were to be taken on board. Course was then to be set for the Thames. This river, and the Medway, were to be entered, and in the latter the men-of-war lying there were to be captured or destroyed. The dockyard installations at Chatham were similarly to be destroyed. Troops were to be landed to capture forts which might hinder these operations and also to make the attack more damaging to the enemy by creating alarm and confusion. Finally, the news of the Dutch fleet's being at sea was to be conveyed to the Governors of Calais and Boulogne, who in turn were to inform the French Government. (This was because on 25 April 1667 France and the United Provinces had made an agreement at The Hague providing for joint naval action against England.)

On 29 May Johan de Witt wrote to Cornelis from Brielle at the mouth of the Maas, whither he had gone to supervise the embarcation of troops and stores. He told his brother that he hoped the expedition against England would be conducted with resolution and crowned with success. There could be no doubt of success, he added, if the ships destined to enter the Medway were commanded with determination and not allowed to withdraw just because they might encounter opposition, or other difficulties. Then, with brotherly admonition, Johan mentioned that he had noticed that

Cornelis was making too much use of the pronoun 'I' in his letters. He advised Cornelis that it was both more modest and more calculated to advance good relations with de Ruyter and other senior commanders if he used 'we' when talking of plans made and decisions taken.

In another letter to Cornelis, also written from Brielle on 29 May, Johan informed him that Dolman had embarked; and in yet another, written this time from The Hague on 31 May, Johan remarked that the English envoys at Breda needed a sharp lesson to curb their arrogance. The men-of-war in the Medway should therefore be captured if possible, and not burnt or destroyed, in order to humiliate the English to the utmost. In yet another letter to Cornelis written on 10 June, Johan commented that the peace negotiations at Breda were not making much headway. He added, imperiously, that he expected from Cornelis, from de Ruyter and from the other leading officers of the fleet deeds which would prove that they were the best plenipotentiaries for peace.[1]

The troops and stores had been taken on board the fleet on 31 May and 1 June, and then it sailed southwards to Schooneveld,[2] off the island of Walcheren, where more troops were embarked. De Ruyter waited here for three more days, in vain, for the Friesland and Zeeland squadrons; but then, without delaying any further, the fleet sailed on 4 June towards England, making for the Thames estuary. The sharp lesson which Johan de Witt felt was necessary to curb English arrogance was about to be administered.

[1] R. Fruin and N. Japikse, *Brieven van Johan de Witt*, Amsterdam, 1912, Vol. III, 1665-9, p. 302.
[2] Shallow water covering sunken land off the mouth of the Western Scheldt.

CHAPTER VI

Great Business in Hand

DURING MAY AND the first few days of June 1667, when the Dutch were getting their fleet ready for sea, the English did not lack for information. This they received from various informants in the United Provinces, either directly or through intermediaries. Towards the end of May reports came in that the Dutch fleet was lying off Texel, and that soldiers were ready to be embarked. On 31 May Dr. Mews, a member of the English peace delegation at Breda, wrote to Joseph Williamson and informed him that the fleet had left the rendezvous off Texel on 27 May, and that from the number of soldiers who had been taken on board it was thought that the Dutch intended a landing somewhere. He added that Dolman

... and all ye gang of Rebells here with ye addition of som malcontents out of Engl^d and Scotland have met in ye Hague. . . . Certain it is they [i.e. the Dutch] have great business in hand; and I presume will very shortly attempt to execute it.[1]

In a letter from Amsterdam, written probably on 1 June, Pierre du Moulin informed Lord Arlington that he had been present when the Dutch fleet left Texel. He said it numbered about sixty men-of-war with fourteen or fifteen fireships, that nine or ten good ships had been left behind, but were soon to rejoin the main fleet, and that the Zeeland squadron was also to follow on. Du Moulin continued:

What their intention is now is kept here very secret onely 't is confidently reported that 20 merchant ships have been hired to follow ye fleet and carry both provisions and men, who they say are ready in ye Mase.[2]

[1] S.P. 84 (182), f. 153.   [2] Ibid., f. 130.

It seems incredible that in face of these and other equally precise warnings, a spirit of what can only be described as fatuous complacency prevailed in Whitehall. Charles II himself seems to have relied with misplaced confidence on Louis XIV to bring pressure on the Dutch to make peace, in accordance with an agreement made in April 1667 between the two kings. But Charles was probably even more convinced that no bellicose move was to be expected from the Dutch after Louis XIV invaded the Spanish Netherlands on 24 May 1667 to pursue his claim that the sovereignty over them had devolved on his wife, a daughter of Philip IV of Spain.

On the very same day Charles wrote to his brother James, Duke of York and Lord High Admiral, informing him that as London was well supplied with coal, and merchant ships had safely returned from the Mediterranean, he had resolved on a further reduction in the number of men-of-war to be kept in service, leaving only a squadron of small ships to disturb Dutch trade. On 29 May Sir William Coventry followed up this royal move in an economy campaign by writing to the Navy Board and asking whether the king's expenses might not be eased by reducing the complements of the fireships lying at Portsmouth, Harwich, Dover, Sheerness, and Chatham. Coventry suggested, indeed, that only sufficient men should be left on board each ship as would be required to weigh anchor, if this should prove necessary.

The king's confidence that the Dutch were bent on peace and could not afford to risk a show of force was shared by his Secretary of State Arlington, who expressed the opinion that the Dutch fleet preparations at the end of May were but a 'bravado', and that they could not afford to prolong the war. Nevertheless, Arlington seems to have felt some apprehension. In a letter written from Whitehall on 5 June 1667 to Sir Robert Southwell, the English Ambassador in Lisbon, he remarked:

The Dutch, now, in this very conjuncture, and at the first entry into the treaty [i.e. the peace negotiations at Breda], have sent their Fleet to Sea, we having no strength to look them in the face; which People will always understand as an Evidence of our Weakness, but I can assure you, upon the maturest consideration of what is past in this War, it was chosen as the wisest course to proceed thus.[1]

The reports that the Dutch had embarked a large number of troops on board their fleet did at least prompt the English Government to take what steps they could to deter, or counter, an attempt at a landing. On 29 May Arlington wrote to each of the Lord Lieutenants of the maritime counties on the East and South-east coasts as follows:

My Lord,
His Majesty understanding that the Dutch are ready in few days to put to sea with their fleet, and believing they will not fail to appear before the coast, to give the alarm to the country, and possibly, if they find the occasion easy, make an attempt to land, with design at least to spoil, burn and sackage what part they can of the country, his Majesty, out of his gracious care for the safety and quiet of his subjects, hath commanded me to give you this notice of it, and to signify to you his pleasure that, forthwith upon receipt hereof, you give order that the militia of that county be in such a readiness that, upon the shortest warning, they may assemble and be in arms for the defence of the coast, in case of any attempt or appearance of the enemy's fleet; taking care in the meantime that the several beacons upon and near the coast be duly watched, by the respective hundreds,[2] in which they are, for the preventing any surprise or sudden descent of the enemy.

And his Majesty commands me particularly to mind you that, in all places where you shall be obliged to make head or appear to the enemy, you make the greatest show you can in numbers, and more especially of horse, even though it be of such as are otherwise wholly unfit and improper for nearer service, horse being the force that will most discourage the enemy from landing, for any such attempt.[3]

On 4 June, a few days after these instructions had been sent out, the Dutch fleet had sailed from Schooneveld. When, however, it reached the English coast, a few miles off the North Foreland on 5 June, a gale sprang up and a number of the ships lost station and were dispersed. Eventually, however, they reassembled, and the fleet was made ready for action. It was a formidable force, comprising fifty-one large men-of-war, three frigates, six armed

[1] *The Right Honourable the Earl of Arlington's Letters to Sir William Temple, July 1665–September 1670*, ed. Thomas Bebington, London, 1701, p. 172.
[2] An administrative sub-division of a county.
[3] C.S.P.D., 1667, p. xii.

yachts, fourteen fireships, and a number of galliotts[1] and other small vessels, bringing the total to about eighty ships. Because of the agreement signed by the French and Dutch in The Hague on 25 April, providing for joint naval operations against England, the Dutch hoped to make the combat force even more imposing by effecting a junction with the French fleet. On 6 June, therefore, Cornelis de Witt sent a message to the Duc de Beaufort, who was in command of the French fleet, informing him of the whereabouts of the Dutch.

On Friday 7 June the fleet sailed into the King's Channel, one of the main approaches to the Thames, and anchored there. In the evening a council of war was held on board the *Zeven Provinciën*, and the instructions of the States-General, detailing the objectives of the operation, which had been revealed to the fleet commanders on 27 May, were now made known to the lesser officers. The conference was resumed on board the *Zeven Provinciën* at 4 a.m. on 8 June, and it was then decided to send a small squadron into the Thames under van Ghent, with Vice-Admiral de Liefde as his second-in-command. The decision was taken because a Norwegian merchantman had been intercepted on its way out of the Thames, and from the skipper the Dutch had learnt that about twenty English merchantmen, attended by some frigates, were lying in Hope Reach just below Gravesend. Van Ghent was ordered to capture or destroy as many of these as possible; but the decision to undertake the operation was made with reluctance by de Ruyter and the other naval commanders. They were, however, overruled by Cornelis de Witt. The plenipotentiary of the States-General was spurred on by his imperious brother Johan's desire for prompt and decisive action; but the naval officers feared, not without reason, that van Ghent's squadron, and indeed the entire Dutch fleet, might find themselves in trouble if English ships suddenly appeared behind them in the Thames Estuary. Sir Jeremy Smith, with some eighteen frigates, was known to be based on the east coast of Scotland, and other small squadrons were reported at Portsmouth, Plymouth and Dover. In case any of these scattered detachments should make an untimely appearance, it

[1] A small vessel of shallow draught.

73

was agreed at the Council of War that de Ruyter should remain with the main body of the fleet at the entrance to the King's Channel, while Vice-Admiral Schram with a small force should keep watch on the Straits of Dover.

At dawn on 9 June van Ghent, accompanied by Cornelis de Witt, and helped by a favourable wind and tide, sailed towards the mouth of the Thames in the *Agatha*, followed by the other ships of his squadron. By evening, however, because the wind had dropped and the tide had turned, he had to anchor at Hole Haven, some eight miles from the Hope. During this enforced halt the Dutch landed some men on Canvey Island, where they burned down barns and houses and killed some sheep to take on board for provisions. They were, however, eventually driven off by the local militia.

The pause in the Dutch operation gave the English time to move the merchantmen higher up the river, above Gravesend, where the Dutch, uncertain of the state of the shore defences, decided it was too risky to press the attack. Frustrated, van Ghent's squadron returned down river, and Cornelis de Witt now decided to concentrate on the major objective of the expedition— the raid on the ships and dockyard installations in the Medway.

The news of the movements of the Dutch fleet at the end of May and beginning of June had soon become public knowledge, for on 27 May an English newsletter had reported: 'The noise of the coming out of the Holland fleet has reached some of our ports.' It continued, with an assurance which events were soon to prove grossly misplaced: '. . . who, by the late care of authority, are provided sufficiently for their security'. On Thursday 30 May the same newsletter stated:

About 4000 land-soldiers are put aboard the Dutch fleet—in order to a designe—who 'tis said are to be carried in a squadron under van Ghent and commanded by Dolman, an Englishman, with whom de Witt had a long conference about that affair. 'Tis the guess there that they intend against Northwards to revenge their former baffle.

Again a note of complacency was sounded, for the writer continued:

Be it where it will we need not question but authority has an eye to their motion, and that they may find another as warm an entertainment, orders being issued forth to all places to put themselves into a posture of defence.[1]

Such confidence that the Government had the situation well in hand was sadly misplaced. After the arrival of the Dutch fleet off the North Foreland on 5 June, reports began to arrive in Whitehall detailing its movements in the Thames Estuary, and these reports should surely have impelled the Government to take drastic action to prepare for the attack which it was now clear the Dutch were likely to make. Yet for three days more, while these reports were coming in, little positive action was taken.

Indeed, on 3 June Sir William Coventry had written to the Navy Board discounting the possibility of a Dutch attack in the Thames. However, he revealed a certain unease by recommending at the same time that an elementary precaution be taken:

We heare by the letters from Holland that the Dutch fleete are certainly abroad, consisting of about 80 men of warre and neare 20 fireshipps, and although I doe not thinke they will make any attempt here in the River, yet it wilbe fitting that ye comand[rs] of the frigatts that are in the Hope be on board to provide against anything may happen.[2]

Pepys recounts in his diary on 5 June how low the morale of the Navy had sunk at this critical juncture.

Captain Perriman brings us word how the *Happy Returne*'s crew below in the Hope, ordered to carry the Portugal Embassador to Holland (and the Embassador, I think, on board) refuse to go till paid; and by their example two or three more ships are in a mutiny: which is a sad consideration while so many of the enemy's ships are at this day triumphing in the sea.

Meanwhile the Duke of York had ordered the Navy Board to give the alarm to the dockyards that the Dutch and French fleets were abroad; and on 6 June Peter Pett wrote to the Board from Chatham, to say that the alarm 'hath been intimated to all persons in this river, who, I hope, will strictly look to their dutys'.[3]

[1] 'Draft Newsletters of Henry Muddiman', *Notes and Queries*, 11 April 1936, Part I, pp. 254–8.
[2] S.P. 46 (136), f. 481.
[3] Ibid., f. 483.

On 7 June reports were sent to Whitehall that the Dutch had been sighted off the North Foreland, and later, in the King's Channel; but even now, when it should have been clear that some enterprise was about to be attempted in the neighbourhood of the Thames Estuary, or in the river itself, the Government took no decisive action. Perhaps this was because it still believed that the movements of the Dutch fleet were a feint, and that the peace was as good as concluded. It is significant that on 7 June Henry Coventry, one of the English plenipotentiaries at Breda, came to Dover in a Dutch vessel flying a white flag. He brought with him provisional articles of the peace for King Charles's approval; but royal consideration of these was to be deferred by the gathering momentum of the Dutch fleet's operations in the Thames and Medway.

On 9 June, the day of van Ghent's abortive sally up to the Hope, English counter-measures were still quite inadequate. Sir William Coventry wrote to the Navy Board that day informing them that the King thought the best way of hindering the Dutch fleet would be to employ fireships, and that inquiries were to be made at once to find out which vessels lying in the Thames could be used for the purpose. Great speed, Coventry added, was essential in securing these ships.

By the morning of 10 June reports had come in that the Dutch had sailed up the Thames towards the Hope, and at last a sense of danger was reflected in measures now tardily taken, and letters which passed. The King ordered the Duke of Albemarle to go to Chatham to take charge there, and three days later he ordered Prince Rupert to Woolwich to organize defences. Pepys recorded in his diary on 10 June how he and other members of the Navy Board went to Whitehall and there met Sir William Coventry, 'who presses all that is possible for fireships. . . . So we all down to Deptford, and pitched upon ships and set men to work, but Lord! to see how backwardly things move at this pinch.'

On 11 June Coventry was still agitatedly pressing for fireships, and in a letter to the Navy Board he lamented the unpatriotic attitude of some shipowners who were refusing to put their vessels at the disposal of the Government for conversion into fireships:

For God's sake get what you can of all sorts for fireships, and send them down as fast as you can lower into the river. If money or any other encouragements will procure men and give despatch, pray spare not.

In another letter to the Navy Board, Coventry declared:

I believe that at this time, which is no less than invasion, His Majesty may by law use any man's ships or goods for public defence, and any resisting will be adjudged criminals; but I hope better temper will be found. If men cannot otherwise be had to serve in the fireships they must be tempted with profit, and even ready money given....[1]

The general panic caused by the appearance of the Dutch in the Thames was manifested in a deplorable way in Gravesend. Pepys related in his diary on 10 June:

Down to Gravesend, where I find the Duke of Albemarle just come, with a great many idle lords and gentlemen, with their pistols and fooleries; and the bulworke not able to have stood half an hour had they [i.e. the Dutch] come up; but the Dutch are fallen down from the Hope, and Shell-haven, as low as Sheerenesse, and we do plainly at this time hear the guns play. . . . I find the town had removed most of their goods out of the town, for fear of the Dutch coming up to them; and from Sir John Griffen[2] that last night there was not twelve men to be got in the town to defend it. . . .

In a letter to Sir William Coventry written at 1 a.m. on 11 June, Pepys described how he sailed down the Thames to Gravesend, and he continued: 'I mett severall vessells in my going downe, loaden with the Goods of the people of Gravesend. Such was theire fright . . .'[3]

On 10 June, a few hours before Pepys's letter was written, Peter Pett had sent a message to the Navy Board in despairing terms, as follows:

Gen:

There is now appeareing at ye Buoy of ye Norre uppward of twenty Saile of Hollenders more, ye one of wch Seames to be a very great Shipp, I feare they will gitt within Sheer Nasse this Eveing, there being little to interrupt them, and doe beleive ye whole Stresse of ye businesse will lie at ye Chain a little beyond Gillingham (where wee

---

[1] C.S.P.D., Addenda, 1660–85, p. 190.
[2] Sir John Griffiths, Governor of Gravesend Fort.
[3] National Maritime Museum MS. LBK/8, f. 491.

have moared to interrupt them as much as wee can from comeing to ye chain) (four great Stages). I wish wee had some of your number to helpe advise and Act in these necessitus times, and y^t you come not too late. . . .[1]

The event which had prompted Pett to send his despairing letter was the arrival off Sheerness of van Ghent's squadron returning from its unsuccessful foray up the Thames. The ships appeared off the Isle of Sheppey about midday on Monday 10 June, and the Dutch at once decided to mount an attack on Sheerness Fort. Captain Jan van Brakel in the *Vrede*, followed by two other men-of-war, was ordered to sail as close to the fort as possible and engage it with cannon fire. The other ships of the squadron were to follow, and under the covering fire troops were to be disembarked to attack the fort.

The opposition encountered by the Dutch was slight. Sir Edward Spragge, an Irishman with long and successful experience at sea, who had taken part in the Battle of Lowestoft, the Four Days' Battle, and the battle on St. James's Day, had been put in command of the ships lying in the Medway and the few small vessels including fireships and ketches which had been posted off Sheerness. The only ship there which was capable of offering opposition to the Dutch was the frigate *Unity*, which had been stationed off the fort to act as a guardship.

At about 4 p.m. on Sunday 9 June, when he had been off Sheerness in the *Henrietta* yacht, Spragge had observed van Ghent's squadron sailing up the Thames Estuary, and he at once put back to Sheerness. Here he sent orders that the *Monmouth*, which was lying at anchor in the Medway about half-way between Sheerness and Gillingham, should be got under way at once and place herself above the chain at Gillingham. Spragge also asked the acting Lord Lieutenant of Kent, the Earl of Middleton,[2] to send to Sheerness the men of a Scottish regiment commanded by Lord George Douglas, who were stationed at Margate.[3]

[1] S.P. 46 (136), f. 488.

[2] The Earl of Winchelsea was the Lord Lieutenant of Kent, but he was serving in 1667 as ambassador at Constantinople.

[3] This regiment became ultimately known as the Royal Scots. One of its companies in 1667 was commanded by a Captain Archibald Douglas, not to be confused with the regimental commander.

The Scots troops were embarked on Sunday night, but were then ordered ashore again, and in the end only one company was sent to Spragge. The latter had meanwhile sent instructions to Peter Pett at Chatham. He was ordered to ensure that the two guardships moored by the chain were fully manned, also that pinnaces and longboats, fully furnished with crews, arms and all necessary equipment, were ready for service on the river. Edward Gregory, Clerk of the Check at Chatham, who had been with Spragge in the *Henrietta*, and who was sent to Chatham with Spragge's orders, was also told to have 100 men from the *Monmouth* sent down to Sheerness as a reinforcement, after the ship had been brought safely above the chain.

These men were embarked at midnight on Sunday 9 June, and the two small vessels which carried them set sail at once for Sheerness. During the night, however, both ran aground, whether by accident or design was never afterwards ascertained, and most of the men took advantage of the opportunity to make for the shore, despite the orders of Lieutenant Kirke, in command of them. When the vessels were finally got off again, only forty-four men remained to continue the journey to Sheerness, the rest having simply taken to their heels.

Gregory returned to Spragge at daybreak on Monday 10 June, and shortly afterwards Spragge sent the *Dolphin* fireship and two ketches to sink the Buoy of the Nore, so that it should not be a help to the Dutch in their navigation. This command was successfully carried out, though the Dutch had stationed a man-of-war, a fireship, and a galliott by the buoy to prevent attempts to sink it. The Dutch vessels offered no resistance to the English, however, and when the latter approached the buoy the Dutch vessels sailed away.

Later that morning some people were observed waving from the Isle of Grain, across the river from Sheerness, so Spragge sent a boat over to investigate. His men were told that some Dutchmen had landed on the Isle of Grain, and help was accordingly requested to deal with them. Despite the slenderness of his own resources Spragge sent over twenty-six musketeers of the Scots company which had joined him, on the understanding that they

79

should be sent back to Sheerness as soon as possible. These men did not return, and so the small garrison at Sheerness was further depleted.

The Kent militia had been called out on 9 June, and during the afternoon of the following day a company of them arrived at Sheerness under command of Major Hugessen. Their quality was so poor, and their morale so low, that Edward Gregory, in a letter to Pepys on 20 July 1667, remarked diplomatically that upon the major's courage and his men's resolution he would undertake to make no comment.[1]

In the late afternoon of Monday, at about 5 p.m., van Ghent's squadron, taking advantage of an incoming tide, approached Sheerness Fort. Captain van Brakel in the *Vrede* was leading, and found the *Unity* frigate with some fireships and ketches lying in their path off Garrison Point, near the uncompleted Sheerness Fort. In this sixteen guns had been mounted, but so very insecurely that when they were fired the recoil drove their carriages into the ground. Seven of the guns were made serviceable by placing loose planks under their carriages to take the recoil, but the fire from these was insufficient to deter van Brakel and his consorts. The *Unity* fired one broadside at the approaching Dutch, but then, when a blazing Dutch fireship bore down on her, she beat a retreat up the Medway, followed by her own fireships and ketches.

Meanwhile the Dutch ships continued to fire on Sheerness Fort, and soon one of the men servicing the guns in the fort was killed, and another had a leg and thigh shot off. The injured man was carried off screaming out loud for a surgeon; and then a rumour spread that no surgeon was available. Thereupon all but seven of the men serving the guns deserted their posts, and shortly afterwards the faithful seven, including Edward Gregory, were also forced to abandon the unequal contest, especially since they learnt that a considerable force of Dutch troops had been put ashore about a mile away.

Gregory and his companions were taken on board Sir Edward Spragge's yacht *Henrietta*, and a discussion took place about what

[1] Rawlinson MS. A. 195, f. 129.

could best be done to hinder the troops whom the Dutch had put ashore. Captain Annesly, one of the gallant seven, was instructed to see whether steps could be taken to flood the marshes in order to obstruct the Dutch if they should try to make for Queensferry and cross from Sheppey to the mainland. As a further precaution Captain Douglas with his company of Scots troops was ordered to station himself at the ferry and remain there till further notice to guard it.

Spragge also sent Gregory off in pursuit of the *Unity* and her accompanying vessels, with orders to tell them to remain at the Mussel Bank, just before the narrow bend where the Medway turns South into Gillingham Reach. Gregory afterwards returned to the *Henrietta* and remained in it with Sir Edward Spragge, watching helplessly while the Dutch continued their cannonade. They did not stop firing till about nine in the evening; and then, Sheerness having been lost, Spragge sailed up the Medway in the *Henrietta* for Chatham.

Long before this the Dutch had captured the abandoned Sheerness Fort. Some 800 men had been landed under command of Colonel Dolman, but a small party of seamen under Cornelis Gerrits Vos, captain of the yacht the *Jonge Prins*, were the first to enter the fort. Disembarking from their long-boat they pulled down the English flag and hoisted the Dutch flag in its place. Cornelis Gerrits Vos later received from the Admiralty of the Maas 100 ducats as a reward for the enterprise which he had shown.

In addition to the guns in the fort, the Dutch found at Sheerness valuable stores, such as sawn timber, masts, spars, quantities of iron and brass, and barrels of gunpowder, resin, and tar. They estimated their value as equivalent to four or five tons of gold (equivalent to 400,000–500,000 guilders); but a later English appraisal calculated their worth, including that of the storehouse buildings, at some £3,000.[1]

After the action of Monday 10 June had ended Cornelis de Witt sat down in his cabin on board the *Agatha* and wrote a letter to the States-General, giving an account of what had happened

[1] Rawlinson MS. A. 195, f. 107.

since he wrote his last letter on 7 June. After telling of the capture of Sheerness Fort, he stated that the guns and as much of the stores as could conveniently be carried in the ships of van Ghent's squadron had been taken aboard, and that he had given orders that what remained on shore should be burned or otherwise destroyed. Cornelis ended his letter, triumphantly: 'From the *Agatha*, lying at the angle of the river of Chatham, before Sheerness Fort, 20 June [i.e. 10 June in the Old Style], late in the evening.'[1]

Some hours later another letter was being written, this time in quite a different vein, by Peter Pett. Late at night on Monday 10 June he wrote to the members of the Navy Board, from Chatham, as follows:

I am sorry I can give you noe better newes then to lett you know that after 2 or 3 howres dispute wth the Dutch by S[r] Edward Sprage Sherenesse is lost. Wee have resolvd the sinkeing of 2 small ffireships in the midst of longe reach to morrow morning the removeing of w[ch] againe I apprehend will be noe great difficultie. Wee shall doe whatever wee can in seruiceing the Navy, and doe wish wee had had some of your assistance in soe great a concerne to his Ma[tie] and the Kingdom.[2]

The implied reproach to the members of the Navy Board revealed that Commissioner Pett was understandably apprehensive of what the Dutch might do next. His fears were justified, for the events of the next few days were to involve him much more closely and directly than the action at Sheerness had done. A situation was in fact developing which proved to be a national disaster.

[1] L. van Aitzema, *Saken van Staet en Oorlogh*, The Hague, 1672, Vol. VI, p. 117.
[2] S.P. 46 (136), f. 489.

CHAPTER VII

The Glorious Arms of Their High Mightinesses

AFTER HE GAVE the alarm on 6 June to the personnel of the dock-yard and the ships in the Medway, Peter Pett does not seem to have taken any positive steps to meet a possible emergency until Sunday 9 June. Even then he had to be spurred on by the orders from Sir Edward Spragge, brought to him on Sunday evening by Edward Gregory. On receipt of Spragge's orders Pett began to issue instructions to the boatswains of ships in the Medway, and to shipwrights in the dockyard. These were ordered to take charge of the pinnaces and long-boats which had been assembled in accor-dance with the Duke of York's instructions of 25 March. These small vessels were necessary for such vital tasks as towing ships, and transporting soldiers, seamen, provisions, stores, and ammuni-tion from place to place. Pett was able to provide a crew (usually numbering from twelve to fifteen men) for each of the boats com-manded by a shipwright; but the boats belonging to the men-of-war in the river, each in charge of the boatswain of the ship, had no crews provided, and the boatswains were left to collect what men they could find. Eleven boats were provided for the ship-wrights, and about 150 men were employed as crews for these. Another nineteen boats, most of which were commanded by boatswains, had scratch crews of seamen, usually very few in number, and no exact record remains of the total number of men employed in these boats. George Moore, boatswain of the *Triumph*, managed to get together thirteen men to man his boat, and the *Vanguard* provided ten for hers, but most of the other boats were insufficiently manned. The boatswain of the *Helver-some*, for example, could find only one man to serve; and the boatswain of the *Rainbow* only two, because the men on board the men-of-war had been ordered to perform other duties.

One of the shipwrights, Thomas Dry, who had been told to take command of a boat, discovered that no boat had been provided for him. Using his own initiative, however, he found a small craft normally used for transporting pitch and tar, and he managed to get some pressed men, who were strangers to him, as a crew. Another shipwright, E. Perkins, was given a crew, but found also that no boat had been provided for him, so he and his men remained in the dockyard, no doubt not unwillingly. In not a single case did the crew of a boat, whether commanded by a shipwright or a boatswain, receive arms. They asked for these, but the reply given was that none were available.

On Sunday night, some of the boats were employed by Peter Pett to take soldiers from the *Monmouth* aboard two hoys[1] which were to take the men to Sheerness, on Sir Edward Spragge's orders. Other boats and pinnaces, also in accordance with Spragge's orders, were directed to tow the *Monmouth* to a position just above the chain at Gillingham; and others again were sent to bring powder and shot from Upnor Castle to the dockyard.

In his two letters of 10 June to the Navy Board, Pett had lamented the absence of senior officials of the Navy, whose help and advice he needed. Soon, however, as the crisis developed, two members of the Navy Board, Sir John Mennes and Lord Brouncker, made their way to Chatham, and early in the morning of Tuesday 11 June, the Duke of Albemarle himself arrived. Under him in positions of authority were, in addition to Mennes and Brouncker, Lord Middleton, Sir Edward Spragge, Lord Douglas, Peter Pett, and the two Masters of Attendance in Chatham Dockyard, Captains John Brooke and William Rand. This proved to be a superfluity of leadership, for as the emergency developed these officials tended to give orders independently of each other. Thus instructions given by one were sometimes countermanded by another, or two sets of conflicting instructions were given. This led to confusion, not to say chaos, and had a bad effect on the already weak morale of the seamen and dockyard-men.

[1] Small coastal vessels.

On Monday 10 June some of the longboats and pinnaces were employed under Pett's direction in transporting soldiers of Lord Douglas's regiment from the dockyard to Upnor Castle and Gillingham. From the latter place they were sent on board the two guardships lying near the chain, the *Charles V* and the *Matthias*. Soldiers were also put aboard the *Royal Charles* and the *Royal James*, lying nearby in Gillingham Reach. Other boats were directed to the chain, where their crews helped to raise it so that a fresh stage could be put under it. One of the shipwrights, Richard Penney, was ordered by Pett to take his boat lower down the Medway in the direction of Sheerness, to try to find out what was happening there. Sheerness Fort had, however, already been taken by the Dutch, and the same evening Sir Edward Spragge, appearing off Gillingham in the *Henrietta* yacht, was able to give full details of the melancholy event.

Spragge joined Lord Middleton on board the *Monmouth*, and discussions at once took place about what should be done to counter a further advance by the Dutch, since it was to be expected that they would without delay make an attempt to destroy the ships and dockyard at Chatham. It was suggested, therefore, that fireships should be sunk at the Mussel Bank, just below the bend of the Medway where the river turns south between Hoo and Darnett Points to enter Gillingham Reach. Spragge was doubtful whether sinking fireships at the Mussel Bank would be effective, since, in his opinion, not enough vessels were available to block completely the two navigable channels near the Mussel Bank.

Despite Spragge's doubts, the project was pursued, after Albemarle had sanctioned it. This he did because Peter Pett had assured him that in his opinion, and that of the two Masters of Attendance, three vessels sunk at the Mussel Bank would be sufficient to stop the advance of the Dutch. Captain Rand, one of the Masters of Attendance, had been ordered early on Tuesday morning to take the *Royal Charles* higher up the river with the help of a pilot. Some shipwrights with their boats and crews were allotted to him to carry out the operation which, from evidence given later by Richard Penney, one of the shipwrights, was ordered by Peter Pett.[1] Rand was, however, subsequently ordered to leave the *Royal Charles*, and to supervise instead the sinking of three small vessels, previously intended for use as fireships, at the Mussel Bank. These vessels were the *Constant John*, the *Unicorn*, and the *John and Sarah*, and Rand successfully carried out his task during the morning of Tuesday 11 June.

Edward Gregory, Clerk of the Check at Chatham, witnessed the sinking of the three ships, and he later described this as 'an unadvised piece of worke'.[2] Shortly after leaving the Mussel Bank he met Lord Brouncker and Peter Pett, who were on their way there, and at their request Gregory went down to the Mussel Bank again with them. He expressed his doubts about the effectiveness of sinking ships there, but these carried no weight with Pett and Brouncker, although they decided that to make sure the blockage was complete more ships should be sunk. Two more fireships (the *Barbados Merchant* and the *Dolphin*), two ketches (the *Edward and Eve* and the *Hind*), and a dogger[3] (the *Fortune*) were accordingly also sunk at the Mussel Bank; but the work was done in haste, since men and boats were wanted for many other urgent tasks that day.

One of the most important of these was to remove higher up the river men-of-war lying in Gillingham Reach. Chief among these were the *Royal Charles* and the *Royal James*, and during the morning of Tuesday 11 June the latter was taken to a new position just above Upnor Castle. The *Royal Charles*, however, which should also have been moved, remained at her moorings. This was because the boats and crews which Peter Pett needed to move her were sent on other tasks, including the sinking of the ships at the Mussel Bank. It seems that these boats and crews, nominated by Pett to move the *Royal Charles*, were taken from that task and commanded elsewhere by the Duke of Albemarle himself. In a report which he made subsequently to the House of Commons he recounted:

He [i.e. Peter Pett] came and told me he would carry her [i.e. the *Royal Charles*] up that tide, if he might have boats, which I could not then

[1] S.P. 46 (136), f. 604.   [2] Rawlinson MS. A. 195, f. 129.
[3] A small two-masted fishing-boat.

spare; for if they were gone, all our batteries must have been neglected, and I could not transport the timber, powder, shot and men to them to resist the enemies the next day. And besides, it was thought advisable, at that instant, if the Dutch should have landed in the marsh by the crane, she [i.e. the *Royal Charles*] might have been useful and have hindered them, having guns aboard.

Nevertheless, upon notice shortly after, that there was neither sponge, ladle, powder nor shot in her, I sent Captain Millett, commander of the *Matthias*, about ten in the morning with orders to Commissioner Pett to carry her up as high as he could, the next tide. Who pretended he could not then do it, because there was but one pilot that would undertake it, and he was employed about sinking ships. And seeing she was not removed in the morning, I myself spake to him, the said Commissioner Pett, in the evening in the presence of Colonel MacNaughton and Captain Mansfeild, to fetch her off that tide. But notwithstanding these orders the ship was not removed. . . . [1]

Further adjustments were made to the chain on Tuesday 11 June. At 1 a.m. Pett had ordered a floating stage to be towed down to Gillingham, and later the chain was heaved up to enable the stage to be placed underneath. The positions of the two guardships lying just above the chain (the *Charles V* and the *Matthias*) were adjusted to enable them to bring their broadsides to bear upon it, and additional soldiers were put aboard them. The *Monmouth* was also moored above the chain, in such a position that she could bring her guns to bear on the gap between the *Charles V* and *Matthias*; and the *Unity*, which had come up from Sheerness too late to be brought above the chain, was moored just below it, as an extra defence.

The Duke of Albemarle, who was at the centre of all this activity, had found a state of crisis at Chatham when he arrived there in the early hours of Tuesday morning 11 June. In his report to the House of Commons he described the situation at Chatham thus:

I found scarce twelve of eight hundred men which were then in the king's pay, in his Majesty's yards; and these so distracted with fear that I could have little or no service from them. I had heard of thirty boats, which were provided by the directions of His Royal Highness [i.e. the Duke of York]; but they were all, except five or six, taken away

---

[1] *Journals of the House of Commons*, Vol. IX, 1667–87.

by those of the yards, who went themselves with them, and sent and took them away by the example of Commissioner Pett, who had the chief command there, and sent away his own goods in some of them. I found no ammunition there but what was in the *Monmouth*, so that I presently sent to Gravesend for the Train[1] to be sent to me, which got thither [i.e. Chatham] about two of the clock the next day [i.e. Wednesday 12 June].

After I had despatched this order I went to visit the chain, which was the next thing to be fortified for the security of the river, where I found no works for the defence of it. I then immediately set soldiers to work for the raising two batteries, for there was no other men to be got; and when I had employed them in it, I found it very difficult to get tools, for Commissioner Pett would not furnish us with above thirty till, by breaking open the stores, we found more. I then directed timber and thick planks[2] to be sent to the batteries, and guns also, that they might be ready to be planted as soon as the batteries were made; and I in the next place sent Captain Vintour with his company to Upnor Castle, which I took to be a place very fit to hinder the enemy from coming forward if they should force the chain. And, upon further consideration, altho' I had horse near the fort, lest the enemy should land there, I commanded Sir Edward Scot with his company for a further strength of the place, and gave him the charge of it, with orders to let me know what he wanted for the security thereof.

Having thus provided for Upnor, I considered where to sink ships without the chain [i.e. below the chain] next to the enemy, as a further security to it . . . advising with Commissioner Pett and the Masters of Attendance, and the pilot, how to do it, Pett told me it was their opinion that if three ships were sunk at the narrow passage by the Mussel Bank, the Dutch fleet could not be able to come up. And I, relying upon their experience, who best knew the river, gave orders accordingly for the doing of it. But when this was done they said they wanted two ships more, which I directed them to take and sink. After this I ordered Sir Edward Spragge to take a boat and sound whether the sinking of those ships would sufficiently secure the passage. Which he did, and found another passage, which the Pilot and Masters of Attendance had not before observed to be deep enough for great ships; but it was deep enough for great ships to come in. I thereupon resolved to sink some ships within [i.e. above] the chain. . . .[3]

[1] Albemarle had, before coming to Chatham, arranged for a train of ten heavy guns to be sent from the Tower of London to Gravesend, to strengthen the defences there.

[2] There was such a scarcity of plank in the dockyard that the floor of the rope-yard was ripped up in a desperate attempt to get material for the batteries (C.S.P.D., 1668-9, p. 582).

[3] *Journals of the House of Commons*, Vol. IX, 1667-87.

Late in the evening of Tuesday 11 June a conference was held in Commissioner Pett's house, attended by Albemarle, Brouncker, and leading dockyard officials including Edward Gregory, to discuss the advisability of sinking ships near the chain. Gregory had discovered the day before, from soundings which he had taken, that the chain was lying nearly nine feet under the surface of the water between the stages, because of its weight. It was presumably because of this discovery that Pett, early in the morning of Tuesday, had ordered a fresh stage to be brought down from the dockyard to enable the chain to be raised higher. Nevertheless Gregory was not satisfied, and remained convinced that the Dutch might have fireships of shallow draught which would be able to ride over the chain. At the conference in Pett's house he proposed therefore that three or four small ships should be sunk in Upnor Reach near the castle, to present a further obstacle to the Dutch should they successfully break through the chain at Gillingham.

After some discussion the Masters of Attendance stated that in their opinion Gregory's proposal was not feasible; but in order further to reinforce the chain it was resolved with Albemarle's agreement that three vessels, the *Marmaduke, Sancta Maria,*[1] and the *Norway Merchant* flyboat should be towed down from the dockyard and sunk as near the chain as possible. Albemarle concluded the conference by ordering Pett and the Masters of Attendance to see to it 'at peril of their lives' that the ships were brought to the chain and sunk there by Wednesday morning. Since it was 11 p.m. on Tuesday when the conference ended, and high tide was due at 1 a.m. on Wednesday, Pett and the two Masters of Attendance were left with little time in which to act. Desperately, they told Edward Gregory to go and search for men who could be used to take the three vessels down the river; but in the prevailing circumstances such a mission seemed doomed to fail. Nevertheless Gregory, undaunted, mounted a horse and scoured the neighbourhood of Chatham for men. By some miracle he managed to collect about 150, whom he brought to the dockyard. They were at once sent aboard the three ships, which

[1] A fine vessel of 70 guns, previously captured from the Dutch, by whom she was known as the *Slot van Honingen.*

were then taken down the river towards the chain at Gillingham.

In Cockham Wood Reach, however, between Upnor and Gillingham, the *Sancta Maria* ran aground, and Phineas Pett alleged later that this was due to the negligence of Captain John Brooke, one of the Masters of Attendance, who was in charge of her. According to Phineas, Brooke wasted time bringing the ship down river, so that the tide ebbed, and the *Sancta Maria*, because of her deep draught, grounded. After unsuccessful attempts to get her afloat again the men aboard her were transferred, some being sent to the *Royal Charles*, others to the batteries at the ends of the chain.

Meanwhile the *Marmaduke* and the *Norway Merchant*, which had been taken down to the chain without mishap, were sunk there about 8 a.m. on Wednesday. A cable was afterwards brought from the *Royal Charles* and fastened between these two ships as an additional hindrance to the Dutch. This was but one of a number of desperate last-minute measures taken under Albemarle's direction. They were prompted by forebodings that the Dutch would not remain content with their easy victory at Sheerness, but would be encouraged by the lack of resistance they had there encountered to venture further up the Medway and attack the ships and dockyard at Chatham. These fears were to prove fully justified.

After the Dutch had captured Sheerness Fort in the late afternoon of Monday 10 June, they decided that because they lacked a sufficient number of troops they could not place a garrison in the fort to hold it. For the same reason they decided also not to venture further inland. Gerard Brandt, the biographer of Admiral de Ruyter, placed indeed another construction on the motives which caused the Dutch to make the latter decision. He affirmed that after taking Sheerness Fort they were well placed to revenge the burning of the fishermen's houses on the island of Terschelling by the English in 1666, by ravaging the Isle of Sheppey. But, Brandt continued: 'They [i.e. the Dutch] wished to act with greater generosity, leaving to barbarous nations this cruel way of waging war and visiting the sins of the guilty upon innocent people.'[1]

[1] G. Brandt, *La Vie de Michel de Ruiter*, Amsterdam, 1698, p. 413.

According to the *Hollandsche Mercurius* (1668), which published extracts from the log-book of Captain van Brakel for June 1667, some of the crew of the *Vrede* ventured into the interior of the Isle of Sheppey, found that the inhabitants had fled, and so plundered their houses and returned with much booty. Another Dutch source, a broadsheet published by N. Visscher in Amsterdam in 1667, which described the Dutch operations during June, stated that a detachment of troops marched to Queenborough after Sheerness Fort had been captured. The inhabitants of the town were said to have begged the Dutch to spare it, and to have offered them 'a considerable sum' of money, whereupon Queenborough was left unmolested. There is, however, no confirmation of this in the Queenborough borough archives, so it may be an exaggeration of some small foray in which the crew of the *Vrede* were concerned. One English account related that the Dutch had marched inland and plundered Queenborough,[1] but gave no details of the operation. A. Daly, the historian of the Isle of Sheppey, stated that the Dutch captured Queenborough after the Mayor had flown the white flag from the town hall,[2] but he did not quote his authority for the statement.

Whatever the Dutch may have done at Queenborough, there is no doubt that some of the unfortunate inhabitants suffered at the hands of the English and Scots troops sent to defend the town. These looted and destroyed goods which they found in houses which their terrified owners had abandoned in fear of the Dutch. Among the townsmen who suffered in this way was Captain Abraham Ansley, a Master of Attendance at Sheerness Dockyard.[3]

On Wednesday morning, 12 June, in accordance with their decision to abandon Sheerness Fort, the Dutch removed the guns, and these were transferred to the ships of van Ghent's squadron. Stores which it was thought worth while to keep were also taken aboard, and the rest were destroyed. Lastly, the fort itself was demolished as completely as was possible within the short time available. The Dutch also expertly destroyed embankments near Sheerness

[1] Rawlinson MS. D. 924, f. 228.
[2] A. A. Daly, *History of the Isle of Sheppey*, London, 1904, p. 224.
[3] C.S.P.D., Addenda, 1660–85, p. 231.

in order to cause inundations; and Lord Brouncker wrote to the Navy Board later, on 22 June, saying that, if the banks were not speedily repaired before the next spring tide, much land would be flooded.[1]

Meanwhile on Tuesday 11 June a small Dutch force comprising two armed yachts (one of them the *Jonge Prins* commanded by the redoubtable Cornelis Gerrits Vos), accompanied by sloops and long-boats, had been sent on reconnaissance up the Medway, to take soundings and also to find out what opposition, if any, the English were preparing to meet a Dutch attack. The little force ventured as far as the Mussel Bank, where they spied the English busy at work sinking the *Constant John*, *Unicorn*, and *John and Sarah* in the South Channel there.

This news, when it was brought back to Cornelis de Witt and van Ghent at Sheerness, did not deter them for one instant from resolving on an immediate attack on Chatham Dockyard and the ships lying in the river near it. These were indeed a tempting prey. In a sketch made by John Evelyn (Pl. IV) on the hill above Gillingham, near the church, and which he sent to Pepys at the latter's request,[2] the names and position of the ships were recorded in detail. The sketch was entitled *A Scheme of the Posture of the Dutch Fleete and Action at Shere-nesse and Chatham 10th 11th and 12th of June 1667 taken upon the place by J.E.* It showed the chain, with the *Unity* moored on the Gillingham side just below it, and with the *Charles V* and *Matthias* moored just above it. The *Monmouth* lay beyond them in Gillingham Reach, and then above her, stretching as far as Rochester Bridge, the *Royal Charles*, *Mary* [*Sancta Maria*], *Royal Oak*, *Loyal London*, *Royal James*, *Catherine*, *Princess*, *Old James*, *Guilden Ryiter* [*Geldersche Ruyter*], *Triumph*, *Rainbow*, *Unicorn*, *Henry*, *Helverson* [*Hilversum*], and *Vanguard*.

Cornelis de Witt and van Ghent decided that a small detachment comprising three frigates, four armed yachts, and two fireships should sail up the Medway forthwith as an advance force, under Captain Thomas Tobiasz., and that the rest of the squadron should follow soon after, under the two leaders. Strict orders were issued that no sailors were to be allowed ashore during the opera-

---

[1] Rawlinson MS. A. 195, f. 150.   [2] Ibid., f. 78.

tion, no doubt to prevent repetitions of the plundering foray of the crew of the *Vrede*, which might have endangered the enterprise.

Tobiasz. and his advance force left Sheerness on Tuesday 11 June, and when they arrived at the Mussel Bank they spent some time moving the ketch *Edward and Eve* which the English had sunk there earlier in the day. This took a considerable time, and meanwhile the tide had ebbed, so the Dutch ships anchored and made no more progress that day. They had, however, freed a passage for the rest of van Ghent's squadron, which left Sheerness about 6 a.m. on Wednesday 12 June, favoured by an east–north–east wind and an incoming tide. When they arrived in Gillingham Reach they found that Tobiasz. and his advance force were held up by the chain, and by fire from the guardships and batteries.

The entire Dutch force was in formation of line astern, partly for tactical reasons, partly because the increasing narrowness of the river made any other alignment difficult and hazardous. In front were the three frigates of the advance guard, with Tobiasz. in the *Bescherming* at the head. Then came the yachts, followed by two fireships, the *Susanna* and *Pro Patria*; and they in turn were followed by other fireships and the remaining men-of-war of van Ghent's squadron. The entire Dutch force, spread out as it was, stretched from a position near the chain to the Mussel Bank, and must have made an impressive sight, especially when the main body approached Gillingham Reach at about 10 a.m.

Because of the narrowness of the fairway, which prevented the Dutch from massing line abreast, their ships were unable to bring a sufficient volume of fire to bear to silence the opposition at the chain, and because of the chain itself they were deterred from sailing on. At this critical juncture, when the enterprise seemed destined to fail, the situation was saved for the Dutch by the bravery of one man. This was Captain Jan van Brakel of the *Vrede* (forty guns, complement 125 men). He was from Rotterdam, and had already given proof of his courage and enterprise in the Four Day's Battle in 1666, and, latterly, during the assault on Sheerness. After this recent exploit, however, he had been put under close arrest in the *Agatha* by order of Cornelis de Witt for having allowed his men to land on the Isle of Sheppey and forage into the interior in search of plunder.

Hearing of the opposition which had been encountered in Gillingham Reach, van Brakel saw a chance of ending his irksome captivity in the *Agatha*. He offered to sail up to the chain in his own ship, the *Vrede*, and while thus drawing the English fire, enable two fireships to be sent against the chain. Cornelis de Witt, in despair, accepted van Brakel's offer, since there appeared to be no alternative but retreat; and so van Brakel was released from arrest and returned to the *Vrede*, which was lying in the rear of the Dutch squadron.

He then carried out an exploit which, both for its daring and its momentous consequences, ranks as one of the most remarkable in the annals of naval warfare. He quickly got the *Vrede* under way, and sailed past the leading Dutch ships, followed by two fireships, until, approaching the chain, he came under heavy fire from the English guardships and batteries. He sailed on, however, and soon there was nothing between him and the chain but the *Unity*, with forty-four guns and some 150 men on board.

Holding his own fire, van Brakel sailed straight for the *Unity*, lying near the shore at the Gillingham end of the chain, and when he was near he fired at her, then came quickly alongside, boarded, and captured her. The opposition from the English ship had been negligible, and this was not surprising in view of the nature of her crew. A number of Thames watermen who had been brought down from London had been sent aboard the *Unity* to complete her complement; but they proved useless. A watch had to be set to prevent them from deserting, and when the Dutch approached, they were the first to abandon ship. Some of the crew who did not manage to escape were taken prisoner, and among these was John Stanley, the ship's surgeon, who three months later, after his return from Dutch captivity, sent in a claim for £32, which he said represented the value of equipment which he had lost when the *Unity* was captured.

The only casualties suffered by the *Vrede* were three men wounded, of whom two later died; and the lack of fighting spirit aboard the *Unity* which this reveals can also be gauged from the fact that earlier in the day Stephen Woolgate, boatswain of the *Great Victory*, had been ordered by Sir Edward Spragge to lie alongside the *Unity* with his long-boat to prevent any of the men aboard her from trying to escape ashore. Woolgate obediently acted as watchdog until he saw the *Vrede* approaching, whereupon he took his boat up an adjacent creek and so avoided capture by the Dutch. For Woolgate the day had been more than usually eventful, largely because of the way in which he was shuttled about as a result of conflicting orders. Early in the day he had been told by Lord Brouncker and Commissioner Pett to go aboard the *Royal Charles*, but was intercepted by Sir Edward Spragge, who told him instead to go and search for seamen ashore, and bring back as many as he could find as quickly as possible. Woolgate returned saying that he had been unable to find any men, and Spragge then asked him what his original orders had been. Woolgate replied that he had been detailed by Brouncker and Pett to go aboard the *Royal Charles* and stay there till further notice. Despite this, Spragge ordered Woolgate to take one of the boats of the *Royal Charles*, man it with some of the crew, and then report to Albemarle for further instructions. Woolgate did this, and after he had carried out a task allotted him by the Duke, he reported back to Spragge; and it was then that he was told to station his boat alongside the *Unity*. Woolgate was one of several boatswains and shipwrights who received orders from one officer only to have them cancelled by another; and this lack of cohesion on the English side, resulting from too many persons giving orders without reference to one another, undoubtedly impeded the preparation of counter-measures against the Dutch.

Meanwhile, as van Brakel was engaging the *Unity*, the first of the two fireships which had followed the *Vrede*, and which was called the *Susanna*, sailed up to the chain but failed to break it, and soon afterwards caught fire. The second fireship, the *Pro Patria*, followed close behind the *Susanna*, rode hard at the chain, and broke it.[1] She then positioned herself alongside the *Matthias*, lying

[1] It is not absolutely certain whether the chain was broken, or whether some of the stages were dislodged, causing the chain to sink, or whether again Dutch sailors landed and let down the chain. Most evidence, however, points to the chain having been broken by the *Pro Patria*.

just above the chain near the Gillingham shore, and set her afire. She burned furiously for a while and then, with a huge detonation, blew up. Some of her crew, including the surgeon, were badly burned, but rescued from the water by the boatswain in charge of the long-boat of the *Triumph*, who was sent by Sir Edward Spragge to pick up survivors.

A third Dutch fireship, the *Delft*, which attempted to place herself alongside the other guardship by the chain, the *Charles V*, on the Hoo side of the river, was sunk by cannon-fire from that ship; but meanwhile another fireship managed to get alongside the *Charles V* and set her on fire. Shortly afterwards van Brakel left the *Unity* in a sloop manned by a few Dutch sailors, and made for the burning *Charles V*. The crew of this vessel were now so demoralized that some of them escaped in boats on seeing the Dutch approach, while others in their panic jumped overboard and began swimming ashore. Those remaining on board surrendered without putting up any opposition when they saw van Brakel climbing up over the bows with his sword drawn, followed by his men clambering over the bulwarks. After the English had handed over their weapons to the Dutch, van Brakel ordered a trumpeter to go aloft and haul down the English flag, and this final humiliation appears to have been too much for the captain of the *Charles V*, who had surrendered with the remnant of his crew. He despairingly tried to escape by diving overboard, but was picked up and brought back on board. The exact number of men taken prisoner on board the *Charles V* is not known; but according to Dutch sources the total of prisoners from the *Charles V* and the *Unity* was fifty-six.

The fire on the *Charles V* took such a hold that the Dutch were unable to put it out and the ship, after burning for the rest of the day, finally blew up. Before this occurred, it seems very probable that she had drifted up the river. In 1876, when new basins were being constructed during extensions to Chatham Dockyard, the remains of an old man-of-war were found at the East end of St. Mary's Creek, with her guns embedded in the mud around her. This wreck may have been either the *Sancta Maria* or the *Charles V*. In a survey of the Medway made on 10 and 11 October 1667 both these ships were reported as lying sunk on the south-east side of Cockham Wood Reach.[1]

After the *Unity* had been taken, the chain broken, and the *Matthias* and *Charles V* set on fire, the *Monmouth*, lying above the chain, had judged it prudent to withdraw higher up the river; she managed to effect this rather inglorious retreat, though she had to be towed by long-boats round the bend of the Medway into Upnor Reach, where she was finally brought to a halt by grounding just above the castle. After some desperate efforts she was got off again, however, and taken still higher up the river to a position opposite the Old Dockyard.

Though the *Monmouth* had escaped, a much more tempting prize still lay in the river a little above the *Monmouth*'s original position. This was the *Royal Charles*, half rigged, and with only thirty-two of her guns still on board. Sir Edward Spragge, foreseeing that the Dutch would try to take her, had ordered the crews of several of the pinnaces and long-boats to go aboard her as reinforcement, and he issued his order 'on pain of death', as was afterwards recorded.[2] Some of the boats' crews were able to escape the unpopular assignment by towing the *Monmouth* into Upnor Reach; the others, who unwillingly boarded the *Royal Charles*, left her promptly soon afterwards when they saw the Dutch drawing near. As they had few, if any arms, these men could hardly be blamed for their dereliction of duty, and in fact Spragge's threat of death for any who refused to go on board and fight does not appear to have been carried out.

There is a story, recounted by Clarendon,[3] that at about this time, when the Dutch broke through the chain, the Duke of Albemarle planned to make a heroic last stand in one of the vessels lying above the chain (perhaps in the *Monmouth* or the *Royal Charles* itself), but was dissuaded from doing so. Clarendon's account was as follows:

The General [i.e. Albemarle] was of a constitution and temper so void of fear, that there could appear no signs of distraction in him: yet it was plain enough that he knew not what orders to give. There were

[1] Sloane MS. 2448, ff. 39–40.
[2] S.P. 46 (136), f. 602.
[3] *The Life of Edward Earl of Clarendon . . . Written by Himself*, Oxford, 1759, p. 420.

two or three ships of the Royal Navy negligently, if not treacherously, left in the river, which might have been very easily drawn into safety, and could be of no imaginable use in the place where they were. Into one of those the General put himself, and invited the young gentlemen who were volunteers to accompany him, which they readily did in great numbers, only with pikes in their hands. But some of his friends whispered to him how unadvised that resolution was, and how desperate, without possibility of success, the whole fleet of the enemy approaching as fast as the tide would enable them. And so he was prevailed with to put himself again on shore: which except he had done, both himself and two or three hundred gentlemen of the nobility and prime gentry of the Kingdom had inevitably perished. . . .

During the action at the chain Lord Brouncker, Sir John Mennes, and Peter Pett assembled as many long-boats and pinnaces as could be gathered together, and stationed them so that they might at least be able to rescue men from the water. As for the three officials themselves, they watched events from a small barge positioned at a safe distance from the conflict. The sight which they must have seen has been described by a historian of the Royal Navy in words which, though picturesque, probably give a fairly accurate picture of what took place:

The scene at that moment to be witnessed below Chatham, has not often been paralleled in naval history. . . . The river was full of moving craft and burning wreckage; the roar of guns was almost continuous; the shrieks of the wounded could be heard even above the noise of battle, the clangour of trumpets, the roll of drums, and the cheers of the Dutch as success after success was won; and above all hung a pall of smoke, illumined only, as night closed in, by the gleam of flames on all sides and the flashes of guns and muskets.[1]

The culmination of this action in Gillingham Reach, and the crowning success for the Dutch, was the capture of the *Royal Charles*, yet this was accomplished without any drama because of the failure of the men aboard to put up any fight. The only dispute, in fact, followed after the ship had been taken, and was amongst the Dutch themselves, as to who had actually captured the ship. From all the available evidence it appears that Captain Thomas Tobiasz. was first aboard the *Royal Charles*, followed by a few men from his sloop, and, shortly afterwards, by others in a

[1] W. L. Clowes, *The Royal Navy: A History*, London, 1898, Vol. II, p. 293.

sloop under command of Lieutenant B. Jacobs, one of the officers of Vice-Admiral de Liefde. Pepys related in his diary on 22 June 1667 that a Captain Hart and Captain Hayward had told him that the Dutch took the *Royal Charles* 'with a boat of nine men who found not a man on board her . . . and presently a man went up and struck the flag and jacke, and a trumpeter sounded upon her "Joan's placket[1] is torn" '.

Amongst the men who had deserted the *Royal Charles* were the boatswain and gunner; they tried afterwards to justify their conduct by affirming that, seeing all was lost, they had tried twice, unsuccessfully, to set the ship on fire before the Dutch reached her. In his report to the House of Commons Albemarle later commented unfavourably on the two men, accusing them of failure to 'do their duties in firing her'.

Beyond the *Royal Charles*, in Cockham Wood Reach, lay the grounded *Sancta Maria*; and she proved to be the final objective of the Dutch on Wednesday 12 June. The crew of a sloop commanded by Captain Jacob Philipsz. of the armed yacht *De Brak* sailed up river and boarded her; but afterwards, in circumstances which were never cleared up, she was set on fire and destroyed by the Dutch themselves. It seems that they did this after all efforts to get the vessel afloat again had failed, but that the decision was taken without reference to Cornelis de Witt.

Long before the capture of the *Sancta Maria* the Dutch had dealt with the two improvised batteries which Albemarle had had constructed at each end of the chain. Concentrated fire was brought to bear on these, and the garrisons, overwhelmed by the sudden onslaught, abandoned their posts and fled. Since the chain had already been broken and the guardships silenced, the way was now clear for the rear ships of van Ghent's squadron to advance further up Gillingham Reach; this they did, led by the *Agatha*, with Cornelis de Witt and van Ghent on board. For a time they transferred to the *Vrede*, to confer with and to congratulate van Brakel, and then they moved on to the captured *Royal Charles*, to discuss on board her what the next phase of the operations should be.

[1] Petticoat.

The *Royal James* and other men-of-war which had been moved higher up the river near Upnor were the obvious targets for a fresh attack; but the tide had ebbed, and it was not possible for the Dutch to follow up their great successes of the Wednesday immediately. They resolved, however, to attack the ships at Upnor as soon as possible the next morning, Thursday 13 June; Cornelis de Witt sent an urgent message to de Ruyter, who was waiting off the Isle of Sheppey with the main body of the fleet, asking him to send more fireships and to come in person up the Medway to confer about the further attack which it was proposed to make.

The industrious Cornelis, remote from all the noisy celebrations which were taking place in the Dutch ships in Gillingham Reach, sat down in the Admiral's Cabin of the *Royal Charles* and wrote to the States-General a detailed account of recent operations. He piously thanked God Almighty, who in His providence had deigned to humble the pride of the English nation by means of the glorious arms of their High Mightinesses the States-General. Cornelis further wished their High Mightinesses much good fortune from the magnificent victory which had been won; and with pardonable pride he dated his letter, at the foot of the last sheet, as follows: 'In the *Royal Charles*, the 22 June [i.e. 12 June Old Style] 1667, about two in the afternoon, lying in the River of Chatham.'[1]

[1] L. van Aitzema, *Saken van Staet en Oorlogh*, The Hague, 1672, Vol. VI, pp. 117–18

CHAPTER VIII

Sad and Troublesome Times

AT 10 a.m. on Wednesday 12 June, when the leading vessels of van Ghent's squadron were entering Gillingham Reach, the Duke of Albemarle watched from the shore, and he witnessed, with a bitterness easily imagined, the subsequent *débâcle* when the Dutch took the *Unity*, broke through the chain, set the *Matthias* and *Charles V* on fire, and captured the *Royal Charles* and *Sancta Maria*. After chronicling this melancholy succession of disasters in the report which he afterwards made to the House of Commons, Albemarle observed, abruptly, 'This was all that I observed of the enemy's action on Wednesday.'

Indeed, he had had too much to do to spend further time in mere observation of the Dutch after they had been brought to a temporary halt by the ebb of the tide on Wednesday. It could be considered a certainty that, spurred on by their successes, they would, as soon as the tide turned, attempt to do further damage higher up the river, where other ships, including the *Royal Oak*, *Loyal London*, and *Royal James* lay, above Upnor Castle. There was also Chatham Dockyard with its storehouses and other installations to tempt the Dutch on.

After the disasters in Gillingham Reach on Wednesday, Albemarle concentrated his energies on providing for the defence of the ships lying further up the Medway, and the dockyard itself. First he inquired of Sir Edward Scott, whom he had put in charge of Upnor Castle, whether it was in a state of preparedness. He received in reply a request for provisions and stores which Scott said he needed urgently, and sent as much as could be carried by the boats and crews still available for transport duties. He also took the precaution of sending an additional company of soldiers to reinforce the garrison, in case the Dutch should try to repeat their exploit at Sheerness by landing and attempting to take the castle by force. As for the three men-of-war lying just above the castle, Albemarle had decided very early on the Wednesday morning that they should be moved towards the Upnor bank of the Medway till they grounded in the shallow water. He then ordered that holes should be cut in their hulls so that it would be impossible for the Dutch, should they reach the ships, to move them. The work of thus immobilizing the *Royal Oak*, *Royal James*, and *Loyal London* had been carried out successfully before the Dutch ceased their operations on Wednesday.

Albemarle's main care, however, was to try to provide some defences for the dockyard, and he ordered three batteries to be constructed, one to defend the Old Dockyard, and the other two the New Dockyard further down the river towards St. Mary's Island. The ten large guns comprising the train of artillery which had just arrived from the Tower of London by way of Gravesend were mounted in a field by the North Crane in the New Dockyard, and about fifty other guns were placed in various positions whence they could bring fire to bear on ships attempting to sail up the river. Many of these guns, including eight which came from the *Old James*, were hastily removed from ships lying higher up the Medway between Rochester Bridge and the dockyard; the eight from the *Old James* were, probably, those installed in one or other of the two former sconces (Bay and Warham), which lay just below Upnor Castle.

Albemarle spent the whole of Wednesday night making these dispositions, and it was a dispiriting experience, for he wrote later in his report:

I stayed all night on the place by the men; and having no money to pay them, all I could do or say was little enough for their encouragement, for I had no assistance from Commissioner Pett, nor no gunners or men to draw on the guns, except the two Masters of Attendance.[1]

Meanwhile the Dutch plans were going forward. In response to the letter sent by Cornelis de Witt, Admiral de Ruyter had left the main body of the Dutch fleet lying off the Isle of Sheppey and had

[1] *Journals of the House of Commons*, Vol. IX, 1667–87.

sailed up the Medway to Gillingham Reach, accompanied by Admiral van Aylua, who had joined the fleet with the Friesland squadron on 11 June, and by Admiral Aert Jansz. van Nes. He arrived in the late afternoon of Wednesday 12 June, after the action of the day had ended, and one of the first duties which he set himself was to go on board the captured *Unity* to congratulate van Brakel on his courage and initiative. Afterwards de Ruyter conferred with Cornelis de Witt and van Ghent about the attack on the ships lying above Upnor Castle which was planned for the next day.

It was decided that four men-of-war and three armed yachts should sail up to Upnor Castle and engage it with their guns, and that under this cover five fireships following them should place themselves alongside the *Royal Oak*, *Royal James*, and *Loyal London* and set them afire. The commanders of the men-of-war were expressly ordered not to venture higher up the river than Upnor, lest they should not be able to withdraw again because of the narrowness of the river there.

Early on Wednesday evening, van Aylua and van Nes sailed back down the Medway to Sheerness, with orders to send without delay all remaining fireships; but de Ruyter, who had decided to take part in the forthcoming operation, slept during the night on board the *Bescherming*, commanded by Captain Thomas Tobiasz., the conqueror of the *Royal Charles*. Early on Thursday morning five additional fireships which had been sent at the request of Cornelis de Witt arrived in Gillingham Reach, so that the Dutch were now in a position to begin their attack on the ships at Upnor.

They were once again favoured with a north-east wind, and it was now merely a question of waiting for the tide to turn, so that they could make use of that also to advance towards Upnor. During the time of waiting Cornelis de Witt and de Ruyter spoke to the commanders of the men-of-war and the fireships, exhorting them to do their duty and to render fearlessly to their country the services which it had a right to expect of them. The commanders, for their part, affirmed their loyalty and patriotism, and promised to do all that lay within their power to carry out their orders. They then dispersed to their ships to await the order to advance.

This came about midday, but by this time the favourable north-east wind had abated somewhat, and this slowed down the progress of the Dutch towards Upnor. They did not in fact reach the castle till about 2 p.m., an interval which gave the garrison time to prepare counter-measures for them. The leading Dutch ships encountered heavy fire, not only from Upnor Castle itself, but also from the batteries on the opposite bank, especially from the heavy guns commanded by Sir Edward Spragge.

In this unpleasant situation the Dutch found inspiration from the presence of their great leader de Ruyter. While the men-of-war and fireships were making their slow progress towards Upnor he had ordered a long-boat to be made ready for himself. When Cornelis de Witt asked him what purpose he had in mind, de Ruyter replied, simply, 'I am going to see what our people will do!' On hearing this de Witt declared that he would accompany de Ruyter, and so they both transferred to the long-boat. During the operation which ensued de Ruyter did not, however, merely sit in the long-boat and watch from a safe distance what happened. He went well forward, scorning all danger in the narrowing fairway, and took an active part in directing operations. Other superior officers, including van Ghent and Vice-Admiral de Liefde, also transferred to sloops and long-boats, and gave orders in the thick of the fire, encouraging particularly the crews of the fireships in their hazardous task.

While the men-of-war were engaging Upnor Castle and the batteries on the opposite bank, the first of the fireships, the *Rotterdam*, grappled the *Loyal London* and set it on fire. Though this ship and the *Royal Oak* and *Royal James* had been sunk in the shallow water by the river bank, enough of their upper works remained above water to enable a fireship to do its work. Two more of these quickly followed the *Rotterdam*, placed themselves alongside the *Royal Oak* and *Royal James*, and soon these vessels also were burning. The fires aboard the *Loyal London* and *Royal James* did not, however, spread as fast as the Dutch desired, and so they sent in their two remaining fireships, one against each of the English men-of-war, and soon the *Loyal London* and *Royal James* were burning as furiously as the *Royal Oak*.

Edward Gregory, Clerk of the Check at Chatham, who had survived the bombardment of Sheerness Fort, witnessed the burning of the three ships, and he wrote later to Pepys, describing the scene.

The destruction of these three stately and glorious ships of ours [he said] was the most dismall spectacle my eyes ever beheld, and itt certainly made the heart of every true Englishman bleede, to see such three Argos's lost. . . .[1]

The noise and confusion of battle must have been even more intense in the narrower confines of Upnor Reach than in the broader waters of Gillingham the day before. The din must have been tremendous, for apart from the guns of the Dutch, there was a continuous cannonade from Upnor Castle, from Sir Edward Spragge's heavy guns opposite, and from other gun emplacements. In the river itself the three large men-of-war lay blazing, sending clouds of smoke billowing upwards, whilst in the middle of the Medway Dutch long-boats and sloops plied hazardously up and down, encouraging their men in the fireships, and evacuating them when their task was done.

The bravery of the Dutch in adventuring thus into these narrow waters under intense fire was astounding, and was rewarded by the demoralizing effect which it had on the men who had been left on board the *Royal James*, *Royal Oak*, and *Loyal London* to defend them. These put up hardly any fight, and the entire operation is redeemed, in English eyes, by the bravery of one man only. This was Captain Archibald Douglas, who with some of his Scots soldiers had been sent on board the *Royal Oak*. When she took fire all aboard her left their posts with the exception of Douglas, who remained, steadfast, till he died in the increasing conflagration.

The bravery of Douglas made a deep impression on contemporaries because of its contrast with the cowardice shown by so many other men, who instead of fighting the Dutch took the first opportunity they could to escape from the scene of action. Sir William Temple, in a letter written to Lord Lisle from Brussels in August 1667, said:

[1] Rawlinson MS. A. 195, f. 131.

I would have been glad to have seen Mr. Cowley, before he died, celebrate Captain Douglas his death, who stood and burnt in one of our ships at Chatham, when his soldiers left him, because it should never be said, a Douglas quitted his post without order. Whether it be wise in men to do such action or no, I am sure it is so in States, to honour them.[1]

The poet Cowley had died in July 1667, but the literary memorial of Douglas which he might otherwise have produced came instead from the pen of Andrew Marvell. He wrote an elegant eulogy of the gallant captain entitled 'The Loyal Scott', a manuscript copy of which is preserved in the British Museum.[2] In this Marvell depicted the last minutes of Douglas on board the burning *Royal Oak* as follows:

> Fixt on his Shipp, he fought the horrid day,
> And wondred much at those whoe ran away ...
> The fatall Barke him boards with grapling fire,
> And softly through its Ports the Dutch retire.
> That pretious life he still disdaines to save,
> Or with known art to try the gentle wave.
> Much him the Glories of his Antient Race
> Inspire, nor could he his own deedes deface.
> And secret joy in his calme brest doth rise,
> That Monck lookes on to see how Doughlas dyes.
> Like a glad lover the fierce flames he meets,
> And tries his first embraces in their sheetts ....
> Downe on the deck he layd himselfe and dyed,
> With his deare sword reposeing by his side.
> And on the flameing plancks he rests his head,
> As one whoe huggs himselfe in a warme bed.
> The Shipp burns downe and with his relicks sinks,
> And the sadd streame beneath his ashes drinks.[3]

The operation against the three ships at Upnor cost the Dutch about fifty men killed and a number (unknown) wounded. These casualties, which much exceeded those of the previous day, were due to the sustained fire from Upnor Castle and the heavy guns

[1] *The Works of Sir William Temple*, London, 1720, Vol. II, p.40.

[2] Sloane MS. 655, f. 18.

[3] More prosaically, in August 1667 Captain Douglas's widow petitioned Charles II to be granted the ship *Golden Hand*, which was employed at the time in raising the sunken ships in the Medway, as compensation for her husband's death on active service.

mounted on the opposite shore which were under the direction of Sir Edward Spragge. These could hardly have failed to do considerable damage to the Dutch because of the shortness of the range, the river being much narrower at Upnor than at Gillingham. The unexpectedly fierce opposition, the first real counterattack which they had experienced, caused the Dutch, once the Upnor operation had been concluded, to abandon any further design which they might have had of venturing still further up the river to attack the dockyard installations and the men-of-war lying below Rochester Bridge. They were also, however, deterred by the fact that they had used all their fireships, and that the river above Upnor was obstructed by a number of vessels which had been sunk or had run aground. They feared, in short, and not without reason, that if they ventured too far they might find themselves trapped in the river with no possibility of escape.

During the attack in Gillingham Reach on Wednesday 12 June, when it seemed very probable that the Dutch would continue their advance without delay against Chatham Dockyard, and the ships lying higher up the river, Albemarle had ordered that all those ships should be sunk at their moorings forthwith. On consideration, however, it was decided that this measure would be too drastic, and instead an order was given that the ships' cables should be cut, and that they should then be manœuvred towards the shore into shallow water and there sunk, so that the Dutch would be unable to remove them should they reach so far. Lord Brouncker, Sir John Mennes, and Peter Pett supervised the execution of this order, and as a result some sixteen men-of-war were cut loose. A few of these subsequently drifted in the river, and thus hindered defence measures against the Dutch, but others were sunk as ordered, for example the *Katherine* just below the New Dockyard, the *St. George* opposite the ropeyard, and the *Victory* opposite St. Mary's Church. The sight of these obstructions in Dockyard Reach was a major factor in deciding the Dutch not to risk any of their ships or men above Upnor, and so the dockyard and the remaining English men-of-war escaped.

On Thursday 13 June, after the Upnor engagement was over and the decision had been taken to go no further, Cornelis de

Witt sat down in his cabin on board the *Agatha* and wrote another letter to the States-General. He recapitulated the events of Wednesday, correcting some of the information he had given in his previous letter, and he then reported on the action off Upnor. He mentioned de Ruyter's arrival on Wednesday, and his part in the operations on Thursday. In these, Cornelis de Witt said, the Dutch had lost no more than fifty men. He then excused himself for not venturing higher up the river. He said that this was considered unwise because of sunken vessels lying in various places, and because English reinforcements were arriving. After commending the officers who had had charge of the Upnor operation for the special zeal and vigilance which they had shown in carrying out their orders, Cornelis ended his letter thus: 'In the ship *Agatha*, lying at anchor in the river of Chatham, before the village of Gillingham, the 23 June [13 June, Old Style] 1667.'[1]

While Cornelis de Witt was engaged in writing his letter Engel de Ruyter, a son of Admiral de Ruyter by his second wife, was sailing up the Medway from Sheerness to join his father off Gillingham. Engel, who was only 18, was serving in the *Hollandia*, but he left his ship in the Thames estuary and sailed up the Medway in a small vessel. He arrived in Gillingham Reach late at night, and as the *Royal Oak*, *Royal James*, and *Loyal London* were still burning off Upnor he ventured higher up the river to take a closer look. Later, in his diary, he recorded his impression and noted down: 'It was a joy to see!' At four o'clock the next morning he went aboard the *Royal Charles*, and after inspecting her with great interest he wrote down in his diary that she was a mighty ship with three decks, and thirty-two guns still in position.

Later in the morning Engel boarded the *Harderwijck*, commanded by Jan Pauwelsz. van Gelder, his step-brother, and there he met his father, Admiral de Ruyter. The latter, with his two sons, joined a landing-party who went ashore during the afternoon in three sloops. During this trip, so Engel later recounted in his diary, planks were removed from a battery which the Dutch had previously destroyed; so it seems probable that the party landed at Gillingham and took the planks from the battery at that

[1] *Hollandsche Mercurius*, Amsterdam, 1668, pp. 84-5.

end of the chain. Engel de Ruyter also recorded that it was during the late afternoon of Friday 14 June that the Dutch left the scene of their victory and began to withdraw down the Medway, assisted by the ebbing tide, and taking with them the *Royal Charles* and the *Unity*. Engel himself sailed in the *Harderwijck*, and then, later, in a sloop in the company of his father and Cornelis de Witt; and during their journey to the mouth of the Medway they met with a Dutch vessel which brought letters for the fleet commanders from the States-General.

The withdrawal down the Medway was not carried out without incident. At various places on the shore detachments of English horse and foot gathered, and these fired on the Dutch ships whenever they could. This intermittent fire made the navigation of the river even more difficult, and just before she reached the Mussel Bank the *Harderwijck*, with de Ruyter himself on board, went aground. She stuck so hard that despite all the efforts of the Dutch she could not be got off, and it was then that de Ruyter, with Cornelis de Witt and Engel, transferred to a sloop in which they continued their voyage. Some other vessels in addition to the *Harderwijck* also grounded, but were got off without difficulty; and the *Harderwijck* herself was later able to resume her withdrawal when the tide turned and floated her again.

The feat of navigation involved in bringing the captured *Royal Charles* down the River Medway in such difficult circumstances won for the Dutch a tribute from the English themselves. In his diary on 22 June 1667 Pepys recounted that two naval officers had informed him that the Dutch carried the *Royal Charles* down the river: 'at a time, both for tides and wind, when the best pilot in Chatham would not have undertaken it, they heeling her on one side to make her draw little water, and so carried her away safe'.

Despite the difficulties which they were meeting in taking their ships down the Medway, the Dutch remained fully masters of the situation, and this they showed when they reached the sunken ships at the Mussel Bank. With remarkable coolness they detached some boats' crews there with orders to burn as much of the upper works of the ships as possible, and this final Parthian manoeuvre was duly carried out. Shortly afterwards the entire Dutch squadron, with their two prizes, entered the broader and safer waters of the Thames Estuary; and there with justifiable satisfaction they fired off their cannon to celebrate the successful conclusion of a difficult and dangerous withdrawal.

The account of the Dutch raid in the Medway, from the taking of Sheerness Fort to the withdrawal on Friday 14 June, as reported in the official *London Gazette* (No. 165, dated 'Whitehall, June 16'), must surely rank as a classic of deliberate understatement. It was as follows:

The Dutch Fleet having the tenth Instant in the evening made themselves masters of Sheerness, on the eleventh they advanced up the River of Medway, and though with much difficulty, passed by several vessels which had been sunk about Musclebank, which was the narrowest part of it, the better to put some stop to them in their passage; and with 22 Sail came up towards the Chain, where the Lord General [i.e. Albemarle] was in person with a considerable force to oppose them; but the Enemy taking advantage of an Easterly Wind and the Tide, which both served them, pressed on; and though their first Ship struck upon the chain, the second broke through it; and notwithstanding a stout resistance in which our Men showed infinite courage, with considerable loss to the enemy, yet they clapt their Fire-ships aboard the *Matthias* and the *Unity*, that lay at an anchor as a Guard to the Chain, and then upon the *Charles the Fifth*, all three of them Dutch ships, that had formerly been taken from them. The same day they possess themselves of the *Royal Charles*, which was twice fired by our Men, and as often quenched by the Enemy.

On Thursday the 13 Instant, about One of the Clock, taking again their advantage of the Wind and Tide, they advanced with six men-of-war and five Fire-ships, and came up towards Upnor-Castle, but were so warmly entertained by Major Scot, who commanded there, and on the other side by Sir Edward Spragg, from the Battery at the Shoare, that after very much Dammage received by them in the shattering of their Ships, in sinking severall of their Long Boats manned out by them, in the great number of their Men kill'd and some Prisoners taken, they were at the last forced to retire, having in this attempt spent in vain two of their Fire-ships which attempted the *Royall Oake*, but were forced off, and burnt down without any effect; but a third had its effect, the two others coming also aboard the *Royall James* and the *Loyall London*, which are much injured by the Fire, but in probability may be again made serviceable, having been sunk before their coming up, and the greater part of them laid under water.

Since then they have not made any considerable Attempt, and by some Prisoners we have taken we finde that the loss we have received has been hitherto so fully returned upon them, that they can have but little reason to Brag of their Success, and less encouragement to make any farther Attempts on these parts.

Part of the Enemies Fleet hath since this Action continued about Muscle-Bank, where on Friday were seen 24 Sail, on Saturday only 14, which 'tis believed stay there only to get off the *Royal Charles*, which is on shoare.[1]

An even more ludicrous attempt to play down the disaster came from the pen of the Earl of Castlemaine, the cuckolded husband of one of the mistresses of Charles II. After asserting that the Medway enterprise had cost the Dutch 'an infinite number of Men and Ten Ships, according to our estimate, although they will not acknowledge so many', the indignant earl considered the loss of the *Royal Charles*:

I confess I was troubled when I heard a ship fell into their hands which his Highness [i.e. the Duke of York] once made use of and had thereby the Honour to wear his Flag; but I was soon again satisfied, when I call'd it to mind, that Sampson himself might be taken by surprize, and that this Vessel could not choose but have an ill end, seeing it had Cromwel for its Founder.[2]

Though the *London Gazette* tried to minimize the magnitude of the humiliating reverse which the nation had just suffered, the panic which gripped London and the home counties as the news of the Dutch advance spread revealed that what had occurred was not a mere incident in a war, but a disaster which was bound to have momentous consequences. Clarendon wrote:

The Distraction and Consternation was so great in Court and City as if the Dutch had been not only Masters of the River, but had really landed an Army of one hundred thousand Men ... if the King's and Duke's personal Composure had not restrained Men from expressing their Fears, there wanted not some who would have advised them to have left the City.[3]

[1] The vessel was almost certainly the *Harderwijck*, and not the *Royal Charles*, which appears to have been brought down the river without any serious difficulty.

[2] *A Short and True Account of the Material Passages in the First War between the English and Dutch since His Majesties Restauration*, London, 2nd edn., 1672, pp. 65, 77.

[3] *The Life of Edward Earl of Clarendon ... Written by Himself*, Oxford, 1759, p. 421.

The stages in the panic are vividly related by Pepys in his diary, and his account is corroborated by other contemporary chroniclers. On 11 June Pepys recorded that he was kept up late trying to provide fireships in response to Sir William Coventry's insistent and despairing demands. Then, wrote Pepys, he went home; he continued:

Where [I had] a great deal of serious talk with my wife about the sad state we are in, and especially from the beating up of drums this night for the train-bands upon pain of death, to appear in arms tomorrow morning, with bullet and powder and money to supply themselves with victuals for a fortnight: which, considering the soldiers drawn out to Chatham and elsewhere, looks as if they had a design to ruin the City and give it up to be undone; which, I hear, makes the sober citizens to think very sadly of things.

On 12 June Pepys wrote:

When I come to Sir W. Coventry's chamber, I find him abroad; but his clerk, Powell, do tell me that ill news is come to Court, of the Dutch breaking the chaine at Chatham; which struck me to the heart. And to White Hall to hear the truth of it; and there going up the Park-stairs I did hear some lacquies speaking of sad news come to Court, saying, there is hardly anybody in the Court but do look as if he cried. . . . Home, where all our hearts do now ake; for the news is true that the Dutch have broke the chaine and burned our ships, and particularly the *Royal Charles*. . . . And the truth is I do fear so much that the whole Kingdom is undone, that I do this night resolve to study with my father and wife what to do with the little that I have in money by me.

Next day, 13 June, Pepys heard 'the sad news confirmed' of the disaster at Chatham, and he wrote:

Which put me into such a fear, that I presently resolved of my father's and wife's going into the country; and at two hours warning they did go by the coach this day, with about £1300 in gold in their night-bag. Pray God give them good passage and good care to hide it when they come home! but my heart is full of fear. They gone, I continued in frights and fear what to do with the rest.

Pepys went on to relate how hundreds of people besieged their bankers in order to withdraw their money, only to be told that twenty days' notice was required. Hearing of this, he resolved after midday to send more of his money ('another 1000 pieces') to

I. A portrait of Peter Pett painted by Peter Lely, with *Sovereign of the Seas* in the background.
(© *National Maritime Museum, Greenwich, London*)

II. Admiral de Ruyter,
by H Berckman.
(*Rijksmuseum, Amsterdam*)

III. George Monk,
Duke of Albemarle,
from the studio of Peter Lely.
(*National Portrait Gallery*)

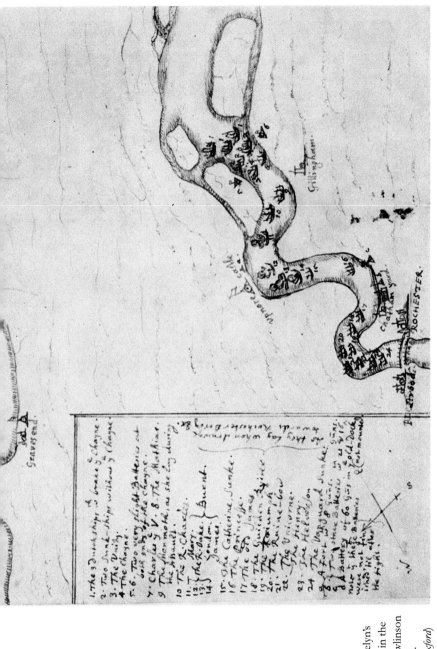

IV. Part of John Evelyn's
sketch of the Dutch in the
Medway, from the Rawlinson
MS. A.195, f. 78.
(Bodleian Library, Oxford)

V. Willem Joseph Baron van
Ghent, by Jan de Baen.
(*Rijksmuseum, Amsterdam*)

VI. Cornelis de Witt,
by Jan de Baen.
(*Rijksmuseum, Amsterdam*)I

VII. The burning of the English fleet off Chatham, by Pieter Cornelisz van Soest.

VIII. The burning of the English fleet in the Medway, by W Schellinks, looking from Sheerness towards Chatham with Rochester in the far distance.

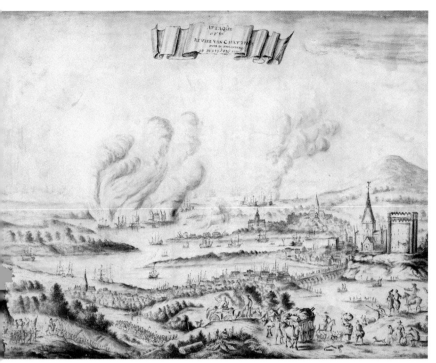

IX. Attack on the river at Chatham, by Bastiaan Stoopendael, looking down
at Rochester to the right. (© *National Maritime Museum, Greenwich, London*)

X. The arrival of the *Royal Charles* in the estuary of the Maas, by Ludolf Bakhuizen.
(© *National Maritime Museum, Greenwich, London*)

XI. Allegorical painting of Cornelis de Witt, by Jan de Baen. (*Rijksmuseum, Amsterdam*)

XII. The sternpiece of the *Royal Charles*, now housed in the Rijksmuseum in Amsterdam. (*Rijksmuseum, Amsterdam*)

his wife 'under colour of an express to Sir Jeremy Smith' who was, Pepys understood, with some ships at Newcastle. He continued:

I also sent (my mind being in pain) Saunders after my wife and father, to overtake them at their night's lodging, to see how matters go with them. In the evening I sent for my cousin Sarah and her husband, who come; and I did deliver them my chest of writings about Brampton[1] and my brother Tom's papers, and my journalls which I value much: and did send my two silver flagons to Kate Joyce's, that so being scattered what I have, something might be saved. I have also made a girdle, by which with some trouble I do carry about me £300 in gold about my body. . . . In the evening comes Mr. Pelling and several others to the office, and tell me that never were people so dejected as they are in the City all over at this day; and do talk most loudly, even treason, as, that we are bought and sold, that we are betrayed by the Papists and others about the King. . . . They look upon us as lost, and remove their families and rich goods in the City.

Pepys concluded a lengthy and dramatic day's entry in his diary by recording: 'I made my will also this day, and did give all I had equally between my father and wife.'

In his entry for the following day, Friday 14 June, Pepys recorded that he had spoken with a Mr. Willson and an employee of Gauden, the Navy's victualler:

who are come from Chatham last night, and saw the three ships burnt, they lying all dry, and boats going from the men-of-war to fire them. But that that he tells me of worst consequence is, that he himself (I think he said) did hear many Englishmen on board the Dutch ships speaking to one another in English; and that they did cry and say 'We did heretofore fight for tickets; now we fight for dollars!' and did ask how such and such a one did, and would commend themselves to them; which is a sad consideration.

Another informant who had been at Chatham, a Mr. Lewes, told Pepys that when the *Royal Charles* was taken some of these renegade Englishmen were heard to say that they had had their tickets countersigned, held them up whilst saying this to prove it, and then declared that they had now come to have them paid, and intended to have them paid before they left.[2]

---

[1] The residence of Pepys's father, in Huntingdonshire.
[2] Because of the lack of ready money and for other reasons it became customary, when a ship was paid off, to give the men certificates from which the wages due to them could

Pepys continued sadly:

Indeed the hearts as well as affections of the seamen are turned away; and in the open streets in Wapping, and up and down, the wives have cried publicly 'This comes of your not paying our husbands. . . .' Most people that I speak with are in doubt how we shall do to secure our seamen from running over to the Dutch; which is a sad but very true consideration at this day.

At the scene of the disaster, Chatham, the spirit prevailing can be gauged from a letter sent on Friday 14 June, by Lord Brouncker and Peter Pett to the Navy Board: 'So heavy is the hand of God now upon this place,' they wrote, 'that we fear it as well as the hand of man now apparently fights against us,' and they went on to declare that after the arrival of the Dutch off Gillingham everybody had believed that 'the whole navy, dock and stores would have been burnt up on Wednesday'.[1]

Pepys' friend and fellow-diarist John Evelyn has also left a record of the general feeling of chaos and disaster which spread as news of the Dutch victories became known. On Tuesday 11 June he wrote:

To Lond: alarm'd by the Dutch, who were falln on our Fleete, at Chatham, by a most audacious enterprise, entering the very river with part of their fleete. . . . This alarme caused me (fearing the Enemie might adventure up the Thames even to Lond, which with ease they might have don, and fired all the vessels in the river too) to send away my best goods, plate etc. from my house to another place; for this alarme was so greate, as put both County and Citty into a panique feare and consternation, such as I hope I shall never see more: for everybody were flying, none knew why or whither.

The state of panic in London was so great that people were ready, on the slenderest evidence, to believe that the Dutch had managed to sail up the Thames to the capital. Thus Evelyn recorded in his diary on Monday 17 June:

This night about 2 a clock some chipps and combustible matter prepared for some fireships, taking flame in Deptford Yard, made such a

be reckoned. On presenting these 'tickets' the men were entitled to be paid in cash; but because of the lack of money delays occurred, and unscrupulous speculators took advantage of the sailors' necessity to cash the tickets at a discount which sometimes amounted to 5s. in the £.

[1] C.S.P.D., Addenda, 1660–85, p. 192.

blace, and caused such an uprore in the Towne, it being given out that the Dutch fleet were come up, and had landed their men, and fired the Towne, as had like to have don much mischiefe, before people would be perswaded to the contrary, and believe in accident. . . . These were sad and troublesome times.

CHAPTER IX

Fruits of Victory

THE NEWS OF the Dutch victory in the Medway reached the United Provinces on 17 June. Johan de Witt, who had that day received from his brother the letters which Cornelis had sent on 10, 12, and 13 June, sat down at once to reply. 'God be praised and thanked,' he said, 'for such a great mercy; and may he grant that the arrogance of the enemy may be curbed, and the present bloody war changed to an honourable and assured peace'.[1] Johan went on to say that after the news had become known services were held in the churches, and the States-General had ordained that Wednesday 26 June should be celebrated as a day of public rejoicing and thanksgiving.

On 19 June, however, in another letter to his brother, Johan expressed the hope, and added that it was the general desire in the United Provinces, that the fleet should try to exploit its recent victories by undertaking further attacks against England. He suggested that perhaps the remaining ships in the Medway, or the ships being built in the Thames at Woolwich and Deptford, might be destroyed. Other possibilities which he mentioned were attacks on the fort at Harwich (Landguard), and the ports of Plymouth and Portsmouth, and the Isle of Wight.

Johan continued his exhortations in another letter written to Cornelis on 23 June. He referred with displeasure to the reluctance shown by the chief officers of the fleet to remain in the Thames Estuary—notified to him in a letter from Cornelis dated 20 June— and he asked why no attack seemed to be contemplated against

---

[1] R. Fruin and N. Japikse, *Brieven van Johan de Witt*, Amsterdam, 1912, Vol. III, 1665-9, p. 306.

Harwich. He strongly recommended his brother to carry out such an attack, also to try another raid up the Thames.

Johan's impatience was hardly justified, for since its withdrawal down the Medway to the Thames Estuary on Friday 14 June the fleet Council of War had been far from inactive. On 15 June it decided that van Ghent should sail north with seventeen men-of-war and some smaller vessels to attack English shipping wherever possible, but primarily to convoy home a fleet of Dutch merchant-men expected from the East Indies. If he had not contacted these ships by 27 July he was to make for the United Provinces, to seek fresh orders from the States-General. The Council of War also decided to detach a small squadron under Vice-Admiral Cornelis Evertsen to cruise between Harwich and the Straits of Dover, with orders likewise to attack any English ships encountered. Finally, Rear-Admiral van der Zaen was ordered to cruise with seven men-of-war between Harwich and the King's Channel, to give the main fleet warning of any hostile ships appearing from the north.

On Sunday 16 June a general service of thanksgiving was held in the fleet for the victory which had been gained in the Medway. Sermons were preached in all the men-of-war, and the main theme of these was that God had clearly been on the side of the Dutch, as had been proved by the favourable winds and tides which he had sent to help them in their endeavours. Brandt, in his life of de Ruyter, recounted that shortly after the thanksgiving had ended, a heavy squall had descended on the fleet. This did not, however, last long; and it was the general feeling that it had been deliberately sent by God to show how such a sudden change of weather could have prevented the Dutch from successfully carrying out their exploit in the Medway, if the Almighty had so desired.

The three squadrons commanded by van Ghent, Evertsen and van der Zaen set sail on 18 June. At the same time Captain van Brakel was detached to take the *Royal Charles* and the *Unity*, first to the island of Goeree, then to Hellevoetsluis. With him went some fifty to seventy Englishmen who had been taken prisoner during the fighting in the Medway. Van Ghent was ordered to give van Brakel the protection of his squadron for part of the crossing, and then, when he was satisfied that the latter would reach Goeree safely, to continue northwards as previously instructed.

On 19 June, before van Ghent's ships had cleared the Thames Estuary, the *Royal Charles* and three other vessels went aground on an ebb-tide, and the rest of the squadron had to anchor awhile until they could be got off. After this inauspicious start, however, the rest of the journey across the North Sea was accomplished uneventfully, and the *Royal Charles* and the *Unity* arrived safely. The *Royal Charles*, which was later moored at Hellevoetsluis, proved an enormous attraction, and thousands of patriotic Dutchmen travelled there to see her and rejoice.

On 18 June the States-General had sent a letter to de Ruyter in which they thanked him for the zeal and courage which he had shown in the recent victorious actions in the Thames and Medway. The States of Holland, too, on 22 June, also wrote to de Ruyter to congratulate and thank him. They added that the States of Holland had decided to have a gold cup made, which was to be presented to him later. The cup, they said, was to be looked on not as a reward, but as a souvenir to be kept in de Ruyter's family, to remind his descendants of the illustrious exploit which the cup commemorated. By the same resolution of 22 June the States of Holland agreed that similar gold cups should be presented to Cornelis de Witt and to van Ghent, and that they too should be formally thanked for the part they had taken in 'the famous expedition of the Rivers of London and Chatham'. The States of Holland concluded their resolution by agreeing that the sum of 72,000 guilders should be expended on the three cups, on which the chief episodes of the Medway raid were to be depicted in coloured enamels.

The States-General did not forget Captain van Brakel, the hero of the attack on the chain. By a resolution passed on 18 June it was ordained that the prize value of the *Unity* should be shared between van Brakel and his crew, and in addition they were granted 12,000 guilders. Van Brakel was also to be presented with a gold chain and medal, together worth 1,200 guilders. The captains of the fireships, on the recommendation of Cornelis de Witt, who testified to their bravery, were also rewarded with sums ranging from 6,000 guilders downwards. Van Ghent, Vice-Admiral de Liefde, Rear-Admiral Vlugh, and Captain Thomas Tobiasz. were each given a gold chain and a gold medal in recognition of the part they had played in the events leading to the capture of the *Royal Charles*.

By a resolution of the States-General on 5 November 1667 it was decided that the guns of the *Royal Charles* or their money equivalent should be allotted as a reward to the men who had captured her. Thereupon a lively dispute broke out, since several officers claimed to have been the first to board her. Vice-Admiral de Liefde was one of these, and his claim was supported by Captain van Brakel, who affirmed that de Liefde's sloop was the only craft which he saw approach the *Royal Charles*. This testimony was corroborated by the officers of de Liefde, who added that Captain Thomas Tobiasz. had approached the *Royal Charles* in his sloop only after de Liefde had boarded her.

Two other officers, Elandt du Bois and Nicolaes Naelhout, also claimed to have taken part in the capture of the *Royal Charles*; but the most convincing testimony was given in support of the claim of Captain Thomas Tobiasz, commander of the *Bescherming*. Men who had served under him during the Medway raid testified on oath before a magistrate that after having cleared a passage for himself by cannon-fire from the *Bescherming*, Tobiasz. transferred to a sloop in which he was rowed up the Medway to the *Royal Charles*. They then declared that he boarded her, and was the first Dutchman to do so. Unfortunately there is no record of how the dispute was resolved; but the guns of the *Royal Charles* were sold in February 1668, and presumably the proceeds of the sale must have been given as prize money to one or other of the claimants.

After the decisions of the Council of War on 15 June de Ruyter had remained in the Thames Estuary with the main body of the fleet, which comprised thirty-eight men-of-war including frigates, four fireships, and a few smaller vessels. Since the Medway victory the fleet had been reinforced by the arrival, at last, of the

Zeeland ships under Lieut.-Admiral Banckert, and on 19 June, because provisions were running short, it was decided to land troops on the Isle of Sheppey again to collect sheep and other livestock. The Dutch traversed most of the island that day, and met with no resistance. Strict orders had been given against unnecessary violence and pillage, and when it was discovered that a few sailors had gone ashore without permission and had broken these regulations, they were severely punished. They were thrown three times into the sea from the end of the main-yard, and afterwards each received 150 lashes into the bargain. Some soldiers of the official landing-party who had also pillaged were punished in like fashion.

The fleet now left the shore of the Isle of Sheppey, and stationed itself just outside the eastern entrance of the King's Channel, whence it kept the Thames blockaded. On Tuesday 25 June, a letter arrived for Cornelis de Witt from the States-General which stated that the effect of the Medway exploit had been very marked in Breda, where the English peace plenipotentiaries had suddenly become much more tractable. But, the letter said, it was necessary that the momentum generated by the success at Chatham should be maintained; and therefore something should be attempted at Harwich, after which the fleet should venture up the Thames again, as far as Gravesend or higher still, in order to keep the English in a constant state of alarm.

The day after this letter arrived was Wednesday 26 June, the day appointed by the States-General for public thanksgiving for the Medway victory. This was duly celebrated throughout the United Provinces by holding services in church, pealing bells, and lastly, in the evening, by firework displays. In the fleet, keeping its watch off the Thames Estuary, de Ruyter ordered the thanksgiving to be observed by firing a number of salutes of guns.

Afterwards a Council of War was held and, no doubt spurred on by Johan de Witt's letter of 23 June, and also by the admonitions of the States-General, the Council decided to send Admiral Banckert with fourteen men-of-war and two fireships up the Thames as far as Gravesend. The squadron sailed at sunrise on

27 June, and anchored later that day just below their objective, having met with no opposition. De Ruyter joined Banckert later with more ships, but they learnt that the river had been blocked higher up by sunken ships, and that many guns had been installed in batteries on the shore. The Dutch therefore decided that it would be profitless to continue their operation, and withdrew during the afternoon of 27 June on the ebbing tide, anchoring in the evening lower down the estuary On 28 June John Evelyn saw them riding at anchor there, and recorded in his diary:

On the 28 I went to Chattham, and thence to view not onely what Mischiefe the Dutch had don, but how triumpantly their whole Fleete lay within the very mouth of the Thames, all from Northforeland, Mergate, even to the Buoy of the Nore, a Dreadful Spectacle as ever any English men saw, and a dishonour never to be wiped off.

On 28 June Count van Hoorne had arrived with reinforcements of troops from the United Provinces, and because of this the Council of War decided to follow Johan de Witt's advice and attack Landguard Fort, which protected the approaches to Harwich. Colonel Dolman with a force of 1,000 soldiers and 400 sailors was put in command of the operation, which the Dutch expected to present little difficulty, since they believed Landguard was weakly held. On 2 July, while ships of the fleet bombarded the fort from the sea, Dolman and his men were put ashore near Felixstowe, a little to the north. They advanced from there on Landguard, accompanied by Cornelis de Witt and de Ruyter, who ventured to within musket-shot range of the fort in an endeavour to inspire the troops by their presence. Sailors with scaling-ladders were sent against the walls of the fort, but met such heavy fire that they threw down their ladders and ran for cover.[1]

Meanwhile English militia had attacked the rearguard left under Count van Hoorne near Felixstowe to protect the boats; and the Dutch force retreating from Landguard were able to

[1] Captain Nathaniell Darell, Governor of Landguard Fort, who was wounded in the action, retrieved one of the ladders afterwards, and it was for many years preserved in the church of Little Chart, Kent, where the Darells had their family seat. It did not, however, survive the destruction of the church by a flying bomb in August 1944.

re-embark only with great difficulty, though according to their own account they lost only seven dead and thirty-four wounded. This reverse, though it interrupted an almost unbroken series of Dutch successes and greatly encouraged the morale of the English, came too late to influence the course of the peace negotiations at Breda.

These, which had dragged on inconclusively for so long, were affected by the Medway disaster, because after that Charles II was in no position to hold out for unduly favourable terms from the Dutch. At the end of June, therefore, provisional agreement was reached, and on 1 July Henry Coventry, one of the English plenipotentiaries, left Breda to seek the approval of Charles II for the articles of peace which had been drawn up. Even now, however, the States-General continued to exert pressure on the English to make sure that the terms would be accepted. On 2 July an order was sent to Cornelis de Witt that, since peace had not yet been definitely concluded, no chance was to be lost of attacking the enemy.

This instruction was received on 5 July, and measures were at once taken to comply with it. The fleet was divided into two squadrons, one of which was put under command of Admiral van Nes, who was ordered to remain in the Thames Estuary to continue the blockade of London. This he did so successfully that the price of seaborne coal and other goods normally brought by sea to London rose steeply in price, causing much hardship in the capital, and fanning the discontent of the citizens, which was already great. The remaining ships of the Dutch fleet, under command of de Ruyter, sailed for the English Channel to do what damage they could along the south coast of England. De Ruyter's progress down the Channel kept the coastal towns in a state of constant alarm, but the only attack made by the Dutch, on 18 July at Torbay, where they entered the harbour of what is now Torquay, did little harm, since they managed only to burn two small merchant vessels.

While de Ruyter was in the Channel the English peace pleni-potentiary, Coventry, had left Deal on 11 July in a Dutch vessel for Breda, bringing the approval of Charles II for the proposed peace terms. The treaty was accordingly signed at Breda on 21 July, but the news of this was some time reaching de Ruyter from Dutch sources. On 29 July his squadron arrived off Plymouth, and the following evening a sloop flying a white flag approached his flagship. Four Englishmen were conducted from the sloop to the admiral's cabin, where they were introduced to Cornelis de Witt and de Ruyter. The Englishmen then informed them that peace had been signed at Breda. Thereupon toasts were drunk to the King of England and to the United Provinces, and the Englishmen offered to send provisions to the Dutch squadron. Cornelis de Witt and de Ruyter declined this offer with thanks, however, since they said they intended to set sail again very shortly. The Englishmen then returned to Plymouth, and on their departure were given a salute of guns by the Dutch, which was returned by one of the Plymouth forts when the sloop reached the shore.

Despite the civilities which had been exchanged, Cornelis de Witt and de Ruyter had decided that the fleet should continue hostilities until news of the signing of peace was received from the United Provinces. Therefore they weighed anchor early in the morning of 31 July, with the intention of cruising westwards as far as the Scilly Islands. While they were under way another vessel was seen approaching from Plymouth, and when it neared the *Zeven Provinciën* a small boat left its side for the Dutch flagship. From the boat stepped one of the Englishmen who had paid the visit of the day before; and this time, after having presented his compliments to de Witt and de Ruyter, he asked them to accept a considerable store of provisions which he had brought with him, including a goat, a quarter of beef, eight sheep, a calf, six ducks, twenty chickens, buckets of eels and fresh salmon, two baskets of fruit, and quantities of fresh vegetables. The Dutch commanders accepted this gift with profuse thanks, and then invited the Englishman to share a meal with them. On his departure, Cornelis handed him a present of money, to be given to the master of the vessel which had brought the Englishman out; after this final exchange of courtesies the Dutch squadron continued its course down the Channel.

Meanwhile, in the Thames Estuary van Nes had received an order sent by the States-General on 18 July to try once again an attack up the River Thames. On 23 July, therefore, he dutifully took his squadron up the river as far as the Hope, but here they ran into a small force of frigates and fireships commanded by Sir Edward Spragge. A short but sharp engagement followed on 24 July in which both sides employed and lost fireships; and the English squadron finally sought refuge by withdrawing to the protection of the forts at Gravesend. The news of the fresh venture of the Dutch into the Thames caused consternation at Whitehall, where it was thought that, as at the beginning of June, a *sortie* up the Thames by the Dutch was but a feint and a preliminary to a major attack on Chatham. Lord Brouncker was therefore sent down to Chatham with all haste; but as events were to prove, the fear of a second attack on Chatham was groundless.

On Thursday 25 July, when the last remaining Dutch fireship ran aground and had to be burnt to save it from falling into English hands, van Nes decided to withdraw. On 26 July, when the Dutch were once more in the Thames Estuary, another small English force of frigates and fireships descended on them, this time from Harwich, under Sir Joseph Jordan. He sent a number of his fireships against the Dutch without effect, and after this the English retired to Harwich, whilst van Nes resumed his station in the King's Channel to continue the blockade of London.

A week after this inconclusive engagement de Ruyter, cruising between Plymouth and Falmouth, at last received, on 3 August, a dispatch from the States-General reporting the signing of the Treaty of Breda. But, the dispatch said, since ratifications of the treaty would not be exchanged for at least a month, and since Article VII of the Treaty provided that hostilities were to cease on different dates in the various parts of the world,[1] the fleet was to continue hostilities until further orders were received, though no more attempts at landing were to be made.

The Dutch squadron under de Ruyter continued to cruise in the Channel till, on 21 August, when the ships were in Mount's

[1] The different dates were necessary because of the difficulty of warning ships at sea in time.

Bay, news was received from the States-General that ratifications of the peace treaty had at last been exchanged at Breda on 14 August, and that peace had been formally proclaimed on the same day. De Ruyter was, however, ordered to remain in the Channel since hostilities under Article VII of the treaty were not due to end in that theatre of war till 26 August; but Cornelis de Witt was recalled, and left the fleet for the United Provinces on 29 August.

On his return he submitted a full report of the campaign to the States-General, and was thanked by them for the zeal and courage which he had shown. Later, de Witt was given a triumphant reception in his native town of Dordrecht, through the streets of which he was drawn in a grand procession, while drums beat and trumpets blared. In the evening Dordrecht was illuminated in his honour, and the following day a long sermon was preached eulogizing the character and services of Cornelis. The town council commissioned a famous painter, Jan de Baen, to paint a large allegorical picture of the Medway exploit, with which the Council Chamber of Dordrecht Town Hall was later embellished. The painting showed, towards the right, the mouth of the Medway with the castle, cathedral, and bridge of Rochester in the background. In the centre the ships set on fire by the Dutch were depicted, and the guns of Sheerness Fort were prominently shown in the foreground, with the Dutch flag flying proudly over them. Cornelis de Witt, holding the baton of command in his hand, was shown seated to the left of this scene, near to a horn of plenty, which represented peace, the fruit of his victory in the Medway. Cornelis was represented as about to be crowned by a flying cherub with the victor's laurel wreath, while a female figure, Peace, was depicted in the top right-hand corner of the painting, blowing triumphantly on a trumpet. An inscription which elucidated the meaning of the painting for viewers stated that it was meant to recall to all generations to come the exploits of the great citizen of Dordrecht who, in an heroic expedition, had destroyed the most powerful ships of England in the very rivers of the enemy kingdom, had taken from her the empire of the seas, and had forced her to make peace.

Much later, in December 1668, the States of Holland awarded

Cornelis de Witt the large sum of 30,000 guilders as a reward for his share in the Dutch victory in the Medway; but this award, in addition to all the other honours which Cornelis de Witt had received, did not win unanimous approval. As it was thought that Johan had brought his influence to bear in deciding the States of Holland to grant such a large sum to his brother, the criticism which the Orangists in particular directed against Cornelis for accepting the money was voiced also against the Grand Pensionary himself.

After Cornelis de Witt had left the fleet to return to the United Provinces, de Ruyter continued to patrol the Channel with his squadron, but more and more men began to fall victims to scurvy; and when on 23 September the ships passed through the Straits of Dover into the North Sea, de Ruyter sent a message to the States-General informing them of the deterioration of conditions in the fleet. He received a reply on 4 October instructing him to return to port; and so at last, on 5 October, the weatherbeaten ships and weary crews set course for Hellevoetsluis, where they anchored later that day.

Cornelis de Witt, on his return, had been received with great honour, and thanked for his services by the States-General, the States of Holland, and the town of Dordrecht. Now it was de Ruyter's turn to receive similar honours. On 7 October he made his report to the States-General at the Hague, and was congratulated and thanked for his initiative and leadership. On 28 October, at a banquet given by the States of Holland, which was attended also by Cornelis de Witt and van Ghent, the three gold cups were formally presented, and de Ruyter and the other two commanders were once again thanked for their services to their country.[1]

In the general atmosphere of rejoicing medals were also struck to commemorate the Medway victory. One of these, which showed the English ships burning in the river, caused great offence to Charles II because the Latin inscription referred to

[1] De Ruyter's cup (just under 12 inches in height) remained in the possession of his descendants till the end of the nineteenth century, when it was acquired by the Rijksmuseum in Amsterdam.

England as a *mala bestia* (a 'brute beast'). The States-General, it is true, did their best to placate the angry monarch by calling in as many medals as possible, and by ordering the destruction of the matrix; but the memory of this medal lingered on in England, and played a part later in renewing the enmity between the two countries.

Another medal was struck by the City of Amsterdam which showed the lion of the Netherlands with cannon between his paws, and with a fleet in the background. The less offensive inscription on this medal was: *Sic fines nostros, leges tutamur et undas* ('It is thus we defend our frontiers, our laws and seas').

The feeling of national pride occasioned in the United Provinces by the Medway victory and the successful termination of the war was also manifested in a number of poems written specially for the occasion. Joachim Oudaen wrote a panegyric entitled: 'Dordrecht's Welcome to its Burgomaster Mr. Cornelis de Witt'. This began: 'City Father, Hero de Witt', and it went on to describe the hero's exploits in the Medway. Another poem by Oudaen, also produced in 1667, bore the title: 'The Humiliation of Britain through the Sea-Power of Their High Mightinesses, under the Command of the Heroic Mr. Cornelis de Witt'.

Joost van den Vondel, the greatest Dutch poet, wrote *The Sea Lion in the Thames*, in which he first recounted that Charles II had boasted of English sea-power; but, Vondel continued:

> Hierop bruist de vloot der Staten
> Naar den Teems, daar Brittenland
> Trots zijn ijzre keten spant:
> Maar wat kan een keten baten
> Als de Leeuw van Holland brullt,
> En de Zee met doodschrik vult?[1]

J. Antonides van der Goes, another celebrated Dutch poet, wrote a piece entitled 'The Thames on Fire' in which he recounted the evil deeds of the 'British wolves', with special reference to Holmes's Bonfire and the destruction of the fishermen's dwellings

---

[1] 'Hereupon the States' Fleet surges towards the Thames. There the British proudly draw across their iron chain. But of what avail is a chain when the Lion of Holland roars, and fills the sea with mortal fear?'

on the island of Terschelling. But, as just reward, so van der Goes said, the English warships, forts and magazines were afterwards all set on fire by the Dutch, to London's eternal sorrow. Van der Goes was also impelled to write a poem which he called: 'On the Gold Cups Presented to Cornelis de Witt, Michiel de Ruyter, and Joseph van Ghent'. In this he referred to the three leaders as the national heroes who had braved the English fire and had frustrated their attempts to coerce the Dutch by means of their sea-power.

The exultation in the United Provinces at this time was intensified by further diplomatic successes which were achieved after the peace of Breda. Because of the general alarm caused by the advance of the French in the Spanish Netherlands, but which was felt particularly in England and the United Provinces, Johan de Witt was able in January 1668 to bring about an alliance of the two countries; the Swedes later joined, making thus a triple alliance. As a result of diplomatic pressure Louis XIV was induced to make peace with Spain in the Treaty of Aix-la-Chapelle in April 1668, and thus a temporary check was imposed on his advance into the Spanish Netherlands.

The treaties of Breda[1] and Aix-la-Chapelle were considered in the United Provinces to represent diplomatic victories which reflected the power and prestige gained by the country under the guidance of Johan de Witt; and a medal was struck to commemorate the national achievement. The medal bore a Latin inscription which proudly recorded that

After having reconciled kings, re-established the freedom of the seas, brought peace on earth by force of arms, and pacified Europe, the States of the United Netherlands caused this medal to be struck, 1668.

During the peace with England which followed the Treaty of Breda Engel de Ruyter, newly promoted to the rank of Captain, though he was not yet 19, was sent to England in command of a frigate to bring back from London the Dutch Ambassador. His ship anchored off Gravesend on 1 July 1668, and he afterwards travelled to London, where he was received at court with much

[1] For the Treaty of Breda see p. 139.

good will. On 22 July King Charles II knighted him, and the same day he left London to rejoin his ship at Gravesend for the return to the United Provinces. Contrary winds delayed the sailing, however, and Engel de Ruyter, impelled by an understandable curiosity, took advantage of the delay to travel incognito to Chatham and Gillingham. Here, as he noted afterwards in his diary, the wrecks of the ships which had been destroyed in the Medway the year before were still to be seen.

The Dutch diplomatic triumph of 1668 proved shortlived. Louis XIV was determined to pursue his campaign of conquest in the Spanish Netherlands, and proceeded, as a preliminary to attacking the Dutch, to isolate them diplomatically. To ensure success an alliance with England was essential, and Louis contrived such an alliance in the Secret Treaty of Dover in May 1670, of which most of Charles II's ministers were kept in ignorance. The Dutch, who had every reason to distrust Louis XIV, strove desperately to placate Charles II in an endeavour to keep him at least neutral in the conflict which threatened with France. The fact that the *Royal Charles* was still moored at Hellevoetsluis as a memorial to the victory in the Medway was a cause of great irritation to the English king. In December 1670 the Admiralty of the Maas decided that the stern-piece, bearing the royal arms, should be removed. This may have been done to appease Charles; but as the vessel itself was left lying at Hellevoetsluis, the gesture did not have any effect.

A year later relations with England had become very strained, and Charles's intentions seemed ominous in the extreme. Sir George Downing, the *bête noire* of the Dutch, had been sent by Charles II to The Hague in 1671 to enlarge on the English grievances, real and imaginary, and the arrival of the envoy was rightly construed as an evil portent in the United Provinces. The role which Downing was cast to play can be deduced from a letter which Charles II himself wrote to the envoy on 16 January 1672, in which he also castigated Downing for not keeping closely to his instructions. Charles wrote:

I have thought fitt to send you my last minde upon the hinge of your whole negotiation, and in my owne hand, that you may likewise know it is your part to obey punctually my orders, instead of putting your selfe to the trouble of finding reasons why you do not do so ...

Charles went on to refer to the question of saluting the flag, and said:

Upon the whole matter you must allwaies know my minde and resolution is, not only to insist upon the haveing my flag saluted even on there very shoare (as it was alwaies practised), but in haveing my dominion of these seas asserted. . . . Notwithstanding all this, I would have you use your skill so to amuse them, that they may not finally despaire of me, and thereby give me time to make my selfe more ready, and leave them more remisse in there preparations.[1]

Shortly after Charles had sent this letter the Admiralty of the Maas decided, in February 1672, to sell the *Royal Charles* for breaking up. It is true that the condition of the ship had deteriorated badly, that it cost more and more to maintain, and that these considerations may have influenced the Admiralty of the Maas; but political factors probably also entered into the decision. The approval of the States-General was not given, however, and shortly afterwards, in March 1672, Charles II declared war on the Dutch in accordance with his undertaking given in the Secret Treaty of Dover.

A year later, when the war was still being waged, the States-General approved a decision, this time of the States of Holland, that the *Royal Charles* ought to be sold for breaking up. In April the ship was accordingly put up for sale at public auction, and was disposed of for 5,000 guilders. As for the stern-piece, it languished forgotten in a storehouse at Hellevoetsluis until, in the middle of the nineteenth century, it was removed to the naval arsenal in Rotterdam. Afterwards it was transferred to the Rijksmuseum at Amsterdam.

Louis XIV had declared war on the United Provinces in March 1672, and the Dutch soon found themselves in a precarious position, for by the end of June the French had advanced as far as Utrecht, and a wide belt of territory had to be flooded in an attempt to stem the French progress. The shock of these catastrophic events in the United Provinces was so great that the

[1] Stowe MS. 142, f. 84.

Orangists were able to whip up popular resentment against the two de Witt brothers, who were made scapegoats for the disaster. On 11 June an attempt was made on the life of Johan de Witt, but he escaped, though badly wounded. Early in July the magnificent painting of Cornelis de Witt which adorned the Council Chamber in the Town Hall of Dordrecht was hacked in pieces, and the part which depicted Cornelis himself was suspended from a gibbet.[1]

A few days later, on 14 July 1672, Cornelis was arrested and incarcerated in the *Gevangenpoort*, a prison in The Hague, on unsubstantiated and almost certainly fabricated charges that he had been involved in a plot against the life of the Prince of Orange. Johan de Witt, who resigned office as Grand Pensionary on 25 July, did all he could to save his brother. He wrote to de Ruyter, and the latter in turn wrote to the States of Holland, testifying to the bravery and integrity of Cornelis de Witt. But in the prevailing mood of the country even de Ruyter could not save his former companion-in-arms.

On 9 August Cornelis was tortured in an unsuccessful attempt to make him confess, and later the same day he was deprived of all his offices and dignities and sentenced to be banished for ever from his native province of Holland. On 10 August Johan visited his brother in the prison, to discuss what should be done; and when this became known a mob gathered outside, and then broke into the prison. When they reached the cell they found Cornelis, still weak from the torture, lying on his bed, while Johan, seated at a table nearby, was reading the Bible to him.

The two brothers were dragged from the cell into the street outside the prison, and there they were murdered in circumstances of hideous brutality. Finally the two bodies, tied back to back, were carried to a nearby gibbet, from which they were suspended by the feet. Even then the savagery of The Hague mob was not assuaged, for later in the evening the two victims were disembowelled and their hearts removed, and various parts of their bodies cut off for grisly souvenirs.

[1] Fortunately a smaller replica of the painting survived, and is preserved in the Rijksmuseum, Amsterdam.

As so often in the past, the United Provinces were saved in their hour of need by the Prince of Orange. Under his direction most of the territory which the French had invaded was won back by the beginning of 1674, and at sea, too, the partnership of de Ruyter and Cornelis Tromp ensured that the English did not gain the supremacy. Faced by this Dutch resistance, and by the unpopularity of the war in England, Charles II was forced to make peace in 1674, and thus brought to an end the third and final Anglo-Dutch war of the seventeenth century.

During the war death claimed two commanders who had played leading parts in the Medway action, one on the Dutch, the other on the English side. Van Ghent was killed in the Battle of Solebay on 28 May 1672; while his old adversary, Sir Edward Spragge, was drowned during the battle of Texel (11 August 1673) whilst transferring from one man-of-war to another.

On 19 April 1676 the great de Ruyter himself died in the Mediterranean whilst supporting the Spaniards against the French. His body was embalmed and brought home and later given a State burial in the New Church in Amsterdam. His death brought to an end a glorious chapter of Dutch naval history: and though the fleet of the United Provinces continued to be an important power-factor in European politics, from now on it declined in strength and effectiveness in relation to the fleets of England and France. Nevertheless, in the Medway campaign in particular the Dutch navy had won for itself and the United Provinces a glory which will never fade. As Pieter Geyl, the Dutch historian, said: 'Never did the Dutch State make a more powerful appearance in the world than in the expedition to Chatham.'[1]

[1] *The Netherlands in the 17th Century*, London, 1964, Part II, 1648–1715, p. 95.

CHAPTER X

Vae Victis

DURING THE MORNING of Thursday 13 June the Duke of Albemarle had received an order from Charles II to return to London. The Duke, however, stayed on at Chatham in view of the critical stage which had been reached in the Dutch attack, and he left only when he was convinced that, since the Dutch had retired after their success at Upnor, the worst was over. He left Chatham about 8 p.m., and arrived in London next morning at 2 a.m., to find the capital in a state of alarm and despair, with rumours and recriminations of all kinds being freely passed around. It was very evident why Charles had recalled Albemarle, who had a reputation for solidity in a crisis.

As the news of the Medway disaster spread to various parts of the country reports came in to Whitehall which revealed how widespread were the feelings of shame and betrayal, and above all of anger, which the reverse had occasioned in all classes of the population. In London the temper of the citizens was additionally enflamed by the sudden steep rise in the price of all seaborne commodities, caused by the Dutch blockade of the Thames.

A letter to Sir Brampton Gurdon, written on 13 June by a correspondent who signed himself 'S.T.', said:

Hon. Sir,
The most lamentable and deplorable Shame that ever was written on any Subject is now my buisenis to give yᵒ upon the utter Ruine and destruction of this pore Kingdom. . . . Our bulwarks are gone, the glory of the nation. . . . We are at this time far more distracted than at the Fire [i.e. of London] . . . The fire was but a flea biting to this.[1]

[1] Nat. Maritime Museum MS. AGC/G1.

James Bentham, writing on 14 June to Joseph Williamson, said:

Reports are that the Dutch have burnt all the King's great ships at Chatham, the men being without ammunition to defend, and have taken one vessel in triumph to Holland. When the news reached London the drums beat, the militia gathered, and there was much running of people. The beacons are on fire, and some say that Harwich, Colchester and Dover are burned, and the King gone out of town or out of the world. There is much whispering of bad persons, and the King and Council are blamed that the ships were left without defence, and that there was no intelligence of the mischief nor care to prevent it.[1]

John Rushworth, writing from London on 15 June 1667, said that the rage of the populace was such that 'people are ready to tear their hair off their heads'; and he added, 'we are betrayed, let it light where it will.'[2] On the same day Richard Watts, writing from Deal to Joseph Williamson, said that when the news of the Dutch victory in the Medway reached the town:

the common people and almost all others ran mad, some crying out we were sold, others that there were traitors in the Council . . . and truly, had not the news suddenly changed, they would undoubtedly have rose and attempted strange things. . . . As it is at and near Deal, it is all the country over.[3]

A letter from Charles Whittington at Hull, dated 16 June, arrived for Williamson and told much the same story: 'We are here', he said, 'much terrified at the unexpected news of the Dutch firing four of our great ships and taking one, and 10 more being in great danger; and some do not stick to say things were better ordered in Cromwell's time.'[4]

Another letter to Williamson, from John Maurice of Minehead, stated:

The moderate and sober people think that there was a great deal of negligence and treachery in this last business. . . . All the Dutch preparations must signify that they had some desperate designs afoot, which was not unknown to all His Majesty's officers concerned in securing the forts and shipping upon the river.[5]

[1] C.S.P.D., 1667, p. 186.   [2] Ibid., p. xxx.   [3] Ibid., p. xxxi.
[4] Ibid., p. xxxiii.   [5] Ibid., p. xxxiv.

Sir Geoffrey Shakerley, writing on 19 June to Williamson from Chester, observed:

The late dishonour received from the Dutch has much perplexed all, and made some say we were asleep, or we should have fortified ourselves against such an attempt, knowing the enemy near. All conclude that there was treachery in the business, and hope the contrivers will receive the reward due to those who betray King and country.[1]

The anger of the London mob was directed in the first instance against Lord Chancellor Clarendon, who had never been in favour of the war, but who was generally disliked. Pepys, in his diary for 14 June, reported that 'some rude people have been . . . at my Lord Chancellor's, where they have cut down the trees before his house and broke his windows; and a gibbet either set up before or painted upon his gate'.

Other persons who were openly accused of treachery included Peter Pett, Sir William Coventry, and Sir Edward Spragge, the last named being referred to as an Irish papist. The king himself did not escape censure, and lost greatly in popularity.

Pepys wrote in his diary on 21 June:

Sir H. Cholmly come to me this day, and tells me the Court is as mad as ever; and that the night the Dutch burned our ships the King did sup with my Lady Castlemaine, at the Duchesse of Monmouth's, and there were all mad in hunting of a poor moth. . . .

Pepys also recounted in his diary on 12 July:

It is strange how everybody do nowadays reflect upon Oliver, and commend him, what brave things he did, and made all the neighbour princes fear him; while here a prince, come in with all the love and prayers and good liking of his people, who have given greater signs of loyalty and willingness to serve him with their estates than ever was done by any people, hath lost all so soon, that it is a miracle what way a man could devise to lose so much in so little time.

Charles II found himself in a desperate position largely because of the utter lack of money with which to carry on the Government at this critical time. He was reduced to such straits that on 21 June he had letters sent to members of the nobility and gentry,

[1] Ibid., p. xxxviii.

135

THE DUTCH IN THE MEDWAY

the clergy and the legal profession, asking them to make voluntary
loans:

Whereas the insolent spirit of our enemies hath prevailed so far with
them as to make an invasion upon this our Kingdom, which is in
continual danger of their attempts upon the same, we hold ourself
obliged to use all fit and proper means both for the repelling of our
said enemies, and the defence of our people.

Charles went on to say that defence could be effected only by
'the speedy raising of a considerable army'; and he therefore
required his loyal subjects to make 'a voluntary liberal advance'
of what sums of money they could afford.[1] On 5 July he sent out
another begging letter, this time to the East India Company, and
in this he declared, frankly:

The exigency of our affairs in this conjuncture being such, and the
difficulties of getting money upon whatsoever funds of credit for the
present so great, we have been obliged to betake ourselves to several
ways of raising a supply for that part of our service which most presses;
and among others, we have thought fit to apply to you for a present
loan of £20,000 for the use of our Navy.[2]

Whilst Charles was thus desperately trying to find means of
meeting his most pressing requirements, attempts were made to
assuage the anger of the people by taking action against those
held to be primarily responsible for the defeat in the Medway.
On 17 June Peter Pett was taken into custody at Chatham by
order of Lord Middleton, and he was sent soon afterwards to the
Tower of London. The news of this disturbed Pepys greatly.
He wrote in his diary on 18 June:

To the Office, and by and by word was brought me that Commissioner
Pett is brought to the Tower, and there laid up close prisoner; which
puts me into a fright, lest they may do the same with us [i.e. the other
members of the Navy Board] as they do with him.

The following day, 19 June, Pepys recounted:

Comes an order from Sir R. Browne [the Lord Mayor of London]
commanding me this afternoon to attend the Council-board with all

[1] C.S.P.D., 1667, p. xl.   [2] Ibid., p. xli.

my books and papers, touching the Medway. I was ready to fear some mischief to myself, though it appears most reasonable that it is to inform them about Commissioner Pett.

Pepys described how he was called before a committee of the Privy Council which included the Duke of Albemarle, Lord Arlington and other notables, and he related:

After Sir W. Coventry's telling them what orders His Royal Highness [i.e. the Duke of York] had made for the safety of the Medway, I told them to their full content what we had done, and showed them our letters. Then was Peter Pett called in, with the Lieutenant of the Tower. He is in his old clothes, and looked most sillily, His charge was chiefly the not carrying up of the great ships, and the using of the boats in carrying away his goods; to which he answered very sillily though his faults to me seem only great omissions.

During the interrogation Pett asserted that he had used only one boat, for the purpose of carrying away his ship models, which were of great value. At this some members of the committee interrupted him to say that they wished the Dutch had captured the models instead of the king's ships. Pett replied sturdily that in his opinion the models would have been of greater value to the Dutch than the ships themselves; whereupon, so Pepys says, all the members of the committee laughed loudly. The general tenor of this first hearing of Pett, when he was baited rather than interrogated, can be judged from a remark of Arlington, made at the beginning of the proceedings. If Pett was not guilty, he declared, the world would think them all guilty.

Not only Pett, but the dockyardmen at Chatham also were made to bear the brunt of the first search for scapegoats. On 14 June Sir William Coventry wrote to the Navy Board informing them that because of Albemarle's complaint that only a few of the dockyardmen had done their duty during the Medway crisis, their wages were to be stopped until their conduct had been inquired into. Sir John Mennes, writing to the Navy Board on 15 June from Chatham, said:

I shall not trouble you with what sad passages we have met with since our coming to this miserable place... here has been much negligence, if not worse, amongst those in this Yard. .... Had we not been totally deserted in the heat of action, and not only by the want of their persons, but bereft of our boats, which were carried away to convey their goods above bridge, far into the country, we might have given a far better account of this place, so wretched now that we can hardly get bread for money.[1]

On Thursday 13 June £9,000 had been sent down to Chatham, the greater part of which Albemarle instructed Sir John Mennes to pay out to the dockyardmen, who had not been paid for fifteen months. On 18 June Lord Brouncker and Sir John Mennes wrote to the Navy Board informing them that the dockyardmen were returning to the Yard, and that because their services were so essential to restore the situation at Chatham, they must be paid wages, and even given a shilling a day extra to encourage them. Brouncker and Mennes declared:

But all this stops not the mouths of the Yard, who have two quarters [i.e. of pay] due to them, and say they deserted not the service but for mere want of bread, not being able to live without their pay. We are fain to give them good words, but doubt whether that will persuade them to stand in the day of trial.[2]

The Duke of York evidently shared the doubts about the dock-yardmen's loyalty expressed by Brouncker and Mennes, for in a letter to the Navy Board on 18 June he said:

Being informed that most of the men belonging to His Maj. Yard at Chatham did desert the service upon the late attempts made by the Enemy, so y^t will not be fitting to relye upon them for performing any service in case the Enemy should make any further attempts in that place.

The Duke then went on to instruct that a sufficient number of seamen should be assembled at Chatham 'for plying the Guns on ye Batteries and for doing any other service that shall shall be necessary for ye preservacion of the Kings ships there'.[3]

Though the Duke of York seems to have thought the seamen more reliable than the dockyardmen, the former were just as discontented as the latter, and primarily for the same reason,

---

[1] C.S.P.D., Addenda, 1660–85, pp. 193–4.   [2] Ibid., p. 196.
[3] Nat. Maritime Museum, *Sergison Papers*, Ser. 78, f. 48.

non-payment of wages. Evidently in an attempt to win the seamen over, an Order in Council on 25 June 1667 appointed a committee including the Duke of York, Prince Rupert, and the Duke of Albemarle, to sit and hear any complaints brought by seamen or soldiers about their pay or conditions of service. Despite measures such as this, however, the temper of the people remained so high that Charles II decided that the only thing to do was to recall Parliament. Pepys shared the general view when, on hearing of the decision on 25 June, he wrote in his diary: 'Great news. . . . The best news I have heard a great while, and will, if anything, save the Kingdom.'

Parliament was ordered to reassemble on 25 July; but four days before it met, the Treaty of Breda was signed. When the news of the Medway exploit reached the English plenipotentiaries at Breda they declared, proudly, that they remained only to await their letters of recall; but in the event Charles II had no alternative but to instruct them to remain and get the best terms they could in the circumstances. It was fortunate for England that at this juncture the Dutch also were willing to make peace, because of the damage the war was doing to their commerce, but also because of the growing danger from the advance of the French troops in the Spanish Netherlands.

For England, therefore, in view of the fact that she had just suffered the humiliating reverse in the Medway, the terms of the Treaty of Breda were far from onerous. Both countries retained the conquests they had made, which meant that England retained New York and New Jersey, although she lost most of her settlements in West Africa. In the East Indies Dutch possession of Surinam and Pularoon was recognized, and England agreed to a modification of the Navigation Act which gave the Dutch carrying trade greater privileges. The English also agreed to a slight modification of the salute at sea, which the Dutch were now required to give only in the English Channel.

Despite the relatively favourable terms, the Treaty of Breda was not well received in England, since it reflected the fact that most of the aims which had prompted the Government to embark on the war had not been realized. The East India Company had finally lost Pularoon, it had received no satisfaction for the damages which it claimed it had sustained in the East Indies at the hands of the Dutch, and the latter had made no concessions to English demands for freedom of trade in West Africa and the East Indies. Pepys recorded the general feelings about the treaty when he wrote in his diary on 23 August 1667 that 'Nobody [is] speaking of the peace with any content or pleasure; but are silent in it, as of a thing they are ashamed of.'

A contemporary broadsheet was produced under the title: *Peace Concluded and Trade Revived in an Honourable Peace betwixt the English and Dutch*. The author of the broadsheet recorded, rather haltingly:

> Now Belgia and Albion shake hands,
> Strongly conjoyn'd together in Loves bands.
> Bones broken, joyn'd together stronger grow;
> I hope England and Holland will do so.[1]

The broadsheet expressed the general feeling of relief that the actual physical strain of the war was over at last; but it did not reflect the prevailing discontent and disillusionment in England, which came to the fore when Parliament reassembled on 25 July. Criticism was directed in particular against a recent decision of Charles II to raise twelve new regiments each of one thousand men, for the defence of the country in case the Dutch should attempt another invasion in the future. The House of Commons feared, however, that this was only a pretext for keeping a standing army in being, and therefore passed a resolution asking the king to disband the regiments as soon as peace was formally concluded.

In view of the temper of the House of Commons, and since the peace treaty had already been signed and merely awaited formal ratification, Charles II decided to avoid further clashes by proroguing Parliament till 10 October. In his speech to both Houses on 29 July he said that he proposed to do this as the emergency was now over; and in dismissing them he declared that he hoped they 'would use all Industry and Severity, for both were necessary, to reduce the People to a better Temper than they have been in of

[1] British Museum, Luttrell Collection, *Proclamations and Broadsides*, Vol. III, No. 96.

late'. Further, he asked plaintively, 'what one thing he had done since his coming into England, to persuade any sober person that he did intend to govern by a standing army'.[1]

The admonitions of Charles II did little to assuage the feelings of discontent and despair which were so widespread, and in which Pepys shared, as his diary entry for 29 July reveals. On that day he wrote:

Thus in all things, in wisdom, courage, force, knowledge of our own streams, and success, the Dutch have the best of us, and do end the war with victory on their side. One thing extraordinary was this day: a man, a Quaker, came naked through the Hall,[2] only very civilly tied about the loins to avoid scandal, and with a chafing-dish of fire and brimstone burning upon his head, did pass through the Hall, crying 'Repent! Repent!' . . . The Kingdom never in so troubled a condition in this world as now; nobody pleased with the peace, and yet nobody daring to wish for the continuation of the war, it being plain that nothing do nor can thrive under us.

Just over a week later, on 8 August, Pepys met John Evelyn, and the two commiserated over the sad state of England: Pepys wrote:

I to my bookseller's where by and by I met Mr. Evelyn, and talked of several things, but particularly of the times; and he tells me that wise men do prepare to remove abroad what they have, for that we must be ruined, our case being past relief, the Kingdom so much in debt, and the King minding nothing but his lust, going two days a week to see my Lady Castlemaine.

The state to which the Government of the country had been brought through sheer lack of funds was reflected in a decision to economize on the Navy. In view of the recent events in the Medway the paramount need was to spend not less, but more, on the fleet; but such was the state of the Exchequer that on 29 July the Duke of York wrote to the Navy Board informing them that as peace had been signed, it was time to consider measures for reducing the royal expenses with regard to the Navy.

The economy campaign does not seem, however, to have

[1] *Journals of the House of Lords*, Vol. XII, 1666–75, 29 July 1667.
[2] Westminster Hall.

hindered the vitally necessary work of repairing and strengthening the defences of the Medway, which had been taken in hand
after the Dutch withdrawal expressly at the wish of Charles II.
On 6 July he had written to Prince Rupert saying that he wished
the Medway to be fortified, in case the Dutch should return. He
ordered him accordingly to go to Chatham, Sheerness, and other
places on the river, to give directions for the completion of
fortifications.

By August 1667, therefore, despite the financial stringency,
some improvement had been made in the Medway defences.
Edward Gregory wrote to Pepys from Chatham on 5 August and
told him that 'a considerable fortification' with thirty guns had
been constructed at Sheerness. In addition two batteries below
Upnor Castle had been fortified with eighteen and ten guns
respectively; another battery of twenty-one guns had been
placed just below the New Dockyard, and two smaller batteries,
of five and eight guns respectively, higher up, whilst a number of
guns had been placed singly in various commanding positions.
Further, so Gregory informed Pepys, a boom had been placed
across the river just below Upnor Castle, near where the battery
of ten guns was located.

This boom consisted of what Gregory described as 'a double
raft of masts'. Behind it was stretched the chain, which had been
brought up from Gillingham; and to strengthen the chain a
cable was slung along it. Both the chain and the cable were supported by stages, and Gregory concluded his account by declaring:

Altogether, as itt is now laied, I believe itt impossible for any ship or
ships to breake through, and conclude no Dutch man will ever have
the courage to attempt itt, being so well protected by the gunnes from
the castle and batteryes wch are indeed excellent workes.[1]

[1] Rawlinson MS. A. 195, f. 118. A chart of the Medway made in 1669 (now in the
collection of the National Maritime Museum) shows two batteries, of 8 and 20 guns
respectively, just to the North of the New Yard. Two more batteries, of 10 and 18 guns
respectively, are shown just below Upnor Castle, and a battery of 30 guns in Cockham
Wood Reach. Broken pales are shown blocking each entrance of St. Mary's Creek, and a
battery of 24 guns is shown at Gillingham, at the entrance of the creek. Finally, a chain is
shown in position just below Gillingham Church. The batteries at Cockham Wood and
Gillingham were designed by Sir Bernard de Gomme, a noted military engineer. Remains
of his battery in Cockham Wood Reach can still be seen.

On 24 August peace was officially proclaimed in London, but this did not close the chapter as far as the Medway defeat was concerned. On 30 August Charles II, both to assuage the popular discontent and to get rid of an adviser whom he felt had outlived his usefulness to him, required Clarendon to surrender the seals of his office as Lord Chancellor. Meanwhile another scapegoat, Peter Pett, was kept a close prisoner in the Tower. Pepys, in the first flush of his indignation, had written in his diary on 13 June that Pett deserved to be hanged for remissness in not carrying out orders given him by the Navy Board. Afterwards, however, Pepys felt compassion for Pett in the latter's plight, and he asked on 22 August if he might be allowed to visit Pett in the Tower. He was told in reply that as Pett was a 'close prisoner' the visit could not be permitted. Thereupon, Pepys recorded in his diary, he put the visit off to another occasion.

The testing time for Pett, and Clarendon, and for Pepys too and many others came when Parliament reassembled in October. The *London Gazette* reported on the ninth of that month that Commissioner Peter Pett, having been twice interrogated before the Privy Council for 'several great neglects in not executing the orders sent to him for the safety and preservation of His Majesties Ships in the River of Chatham', it had been decided on 7 October that a strict inquiry should be held into the whole matter, and that Pett and all other persons concerned should be closely examined.

The House of Commons, which had reassembled on 10 October, needed no prompting to conduct a *post mortem*. On 17 October the House resolved that a committee should be appointed to inquire into 'the miscarriage of affairs in the late war', with authority to send for persons, papers and records. On 23 October, as the *Journal* of the House of Commons records:

The House being informed that it will be necessary to receive some informations from His Highness Prince Rupert, and His Grace the Duke of Albemarle, concerning some miscarriages at Chatham and Sheernesse, and other matters relating to the late war

it was resolved that the prince and the duke should be requested to impart to the committee whatever they knew about any such miscarriages.

Pepys had been ordered to appear before the committee on 21 October, and he recorded dolorously in his diary the night before, 'There is bloody work like to be!' He went on: 'I do see every body is upon his own defence, and spares not to blame another to defend himself; and the same course I shall take. But God knows where it will end!'

Pepys waited at Westminster all afternoon until seven in the evening on 21 October, expecting to be called before the committee. They did eventually summon him, but only to tell him that he would be examined on the next day. In his diary for that day Pepys related that he had 'slept but ill the last part of the night' for fear of what the day might bring. He had no need to worry, however, for he justified himself before the committee. In his own words:

I had a chair brought me to lean my books upon; and so did give them such an account, and so answered all questions given me about it [i.e. the Dutch raid in the Medway] that I did not perceive but that they were fully satisfied with me and the business as to our office [i.e. the Navy Board].

Peter Pett had been present while Pepys defended the Navy Board; and since Pepys had described how various orders had been sent to Pett, the latter was next called upon to defend himself. This he lamentably failed to do. Pepys wrote in his diary:

Commissioner Pett of all men living did make the weakest defence of himself: nothing to the purpose, not to satisfaction, not certain; but sometimes one thing, and sometimes another, sometimes for himself, and sometimes against him; and his greatest failure was (that I observed) from his considering whether the question propounded was his part to answer or no, and the thing to be done was his work to do; the want of which distinction will overthrow him.

On 31 October the narratives which Prince Rupert and the Duke of Albemarle had prepared in answer to the request of the House of Commons were read to the House. Rupert's narrative dealt mainly with the naval events of 1666; but Albemarle concentrated on the Medway débâcle, and in his account of this he laid the chief blame on Peter Pett. He accused him of using boats for his own private purposes, of neglecting to provide sufficient tools, and of providing deal instead of oaken planks for the construction of batteries. In regard to the latter, Albemarle stated that 'as afterwards it appeared' there were plenty of oaken planks in the dockyard, but that Pett had excused himself for sending deal planks by asserting that there were no others. These deal planks, Albemarle said, proved useless, for 'at every shot the wheels [of the guns] sunk through the boards, which put us to a continual trouble to get them out'.[1]

Another serious accusation made by Albemarle was that although Pett had received orders from the Duke of York in March 1667 to take the *Royal Charles* higher up the Medway to a position above the dockyard, he had neglected to do so. Albemarle said that he himself had ordered Pett to have the ship taken up the river, but that the Commissioner demurred, giving as his reason that the only pilot who could safely be entrusted with the task was otherwise employed in sinking ships to block the passage of the Dutch. Albemarle's statement continued:

Seeing she was not removed in the morning, I myself spake to him the said Commissioner Pett in the evening, in the presence of Col. Mac Naughton and Capt. Mansfeild, to fetch her off that tide. But notwithstanding these orders the ship was not removed, but lay there till the enemy took her.

During the evening of Wednesday 12 June, after the Dutch had broken through the chain at Gillingham, and captured the *Royal Charles*, Albemarle said that he directed his efforts towards trying to prepare resistance to the further advance which the Dutch were likely to make on Thursday, when the tide turned. During this critical period, he asserted, he had absolutely no assistance from Peter Pett.

The effect of Albemarle's indictment on the members of the House of Commons was recorded in the Journal of the House as follows:

The House, upon reading the narrative of the Duke of Albemarle, finding Commissioner Pett charged with great and high crimes; and being informed that he was at liberty, walking in the Hall [i.e. Westminster Hall]: ordered that Commissioner Pett be forthwith appre-

[1] *Journals of the House of Commons*, Vol. IX, 1667–87, 31 October 1667.

hended, and brought to the Bar of this House, to answer such matters as shall be demanded of him. Commissioner Pett being accordingly brought to the Bar; and such matters of the narrative of the Duke of Albemarle as did concern him being read, he declared that many of the matters objected against him were new, and desired time to give answer thereunto.[1]

At this point Pett was ordered to withdraw, and the House then resolved that the narratives of Prince Rupert and the Duke of Albemarle should be handed to the committee appointed to inquire into the miscarriages of the war, also that the committee should examine the charges made against Pett. The Lieutenant of the Tower of London was instructed to ensure that Pett was at hand to be questioned whenever that was required.

The committee's report on Pett was submitted on 13 November, and Pepys, who was at Westminster that day, wrote in his diary: 'To Westminster, where I find the House sitting, and in a mighty heat about Commissioner Pett.' As a result of the 'mighty heat' the House resolved the next day, 14 November, that the committee should draw up articles of impeachment against Pett; and on 19 December these were given a first reading. Article I accused him of disobeying the Duke of York's order to remove the *Royal Charles* and other ships in the Medway to places of safety higher up the river. Article II stated that Pett had disobeyed an order of Albemarle to take the *Royal Charles* higher up. Article III alleged that Pett had refused to give orders to Captain Brooke, one of the Masters of Attendance at Chatham, to move the *Royal Charles*, although Brooke had asked for such orders. Article IV accused Pett of misemploying some boats provided for the defence of the river, to carry away his own private property, and of allowing other boats to be thus misemployed. Article V stated that Pett had been so negligent in his duties as Commissioner at Chatham that of 800 men on the books of the dockyard, only ten were available for service when the Dutch came up the Medway. Article VI accused Pett of refusing to supply all the tools required for the construction of batteries, although there were sufficient tools in the dockyard stores for this purpose. Finally,

[1] *Journals of the House of Commons*, Vol. IX, 1667–87, 31 October 1667.

Article VII accused Pett of supplying deal planks instead of the oaken planks which had been asked for, to be used in the construction of batteries, 'notwithstanding that there were in His Majesty's Yard there, several oaken planks fit for their service'.

The House agreed to all these articles of impeachment save Article IV, which was accordingly struck out. Afterwards a petition from Peter Pett was read to the House, asking that he be released from his imprisonment on bail. The Commons agreed, provided that the Privy Council raised no objection; and so Pett was duly released from the Tower of London on 20 December 1667, on bail of £5,000 which was put up by two sureties, Rowland Crispe of Chatham and Samuel Hall of London.

It was while Pett was being examined by the Privy Council and the committee of the House of Commons, and when popular rancour against him was at its height, that Andrew Marvell epitomized the fury of the people and their desire to make Pett the scapegoat, in his poem 'The Last Instructions to a Painter'. In this he lampooned the unfortunate Pett in vitriolic couplets which perfectly reflected the insensate determination to wreak vengeance on the Commissioner of Chatham Dockyard for the humiliation of the Medway defeat.

After a preliminary scourging of Lord St. Albans, Charles II's mistress the Countess of Castlemaine, and the cabal of ministers of the Crown, Marvell turned his attention to the events in the Medway:

> Ruyter forthwith a Squadron does untack,
> They sail securely through the Rivers track.
> An English Pilot too (O Shame, O Sin!)
> Cheated of Pay, was he that show'd them in.
> Our wretched Ships within their Fate attend,
> And all our hopes now on frail Chain depend:
> Engine so slight to guard us from the Sea,
> It fitter seem'd to captivate a Flea . . .
> Our Seamen, whom no Dangers shape could fright,
> Unpaid, refuse to mount our Ships for Spight;
> Or to their fellows swim on board the Dutch,
> Which show the tempting metal in their clutch. . . .
> Now (nothing more at Chatham left to burn),
> The Holland Squadron leisurely return,

And spight of Ruperts and of Albemarles
To Ruyters Triumph lead the captive *Charles* . . .
After this loss, to rellish discontent,
Someone must be accus'd by Punishment. [1]
All our miscarriages on Pett must fall:
His name alone seems fit to answer all.
Whose Counsel first did this mad War beget?
Who all Commands sold thro' the Navy? *Pett.*
Who would not follow when the Dutch were bet? . . .
Who all our Seamen cheated of their Debt?
And all our Prizes, who did swallow? *Pett*
Who did advise no Navy out to set?
And who the Forts left unrepair'd? *Pett.*
Who to supply with Powder did forget,
Languard, Sheerness, Gravesend and Upnor? *Pett.*
Who all our Ships expos'd in Chathams Net?
Who should it be but the Phanatick *Pett.*
Pett, the Sea Architect, in making Ships,
Was the first cause of all these Naval slips:
Had he not built, none of these faults had bin;
If no Creation, there had been no Sin. . . .

Apart from Pett, popular anger was chiefly directed against Clarendon, and after Charles II had required him to retire from the office of Lord Chancellor it was certain that the House of Commons, where he had few friends, would proceed against him. On 16 November the House decided that there were grounds for charging him with High Treason, and requested the House of Lords to commit him to prison. The House of Lords refused to do this, however, until the charges against Clarendon had been made more explicit, and Clarendon himself put up a brave show in the House in his own defence. Afterwards, however, he fled to France; and Parliament had its vengeance in the end by passing an act which banished him for life.

In addition to the general mismanagement at Chatham alleged to be due to Peter Pett, the conduct of naval affairs by the Navy Board had been brought into question, particularly with regard to the scandals of payment (or rather, non-payment) of seamen by the ticket system. On 5 March 1668 the House of Commons

---

[1] Some versions of the poem have 'Parliament'. 'Punishment' is, however, considered to be the original and authentic form.

assembled to hear what the members of the Navy Board had to say in their defence; and on this occasion Pepys, who acted as spokesman for his colleagues as well as for himself, excelled himself. In his diary he recorded:

To Westminster, where I found myself come time enough, and my brethren all ready. But I full of thoughts and trouble touching the issue of this day: and to comfort myself did go to the Dog and drink half-a-pint of mulled sack, and in the hall did drink a dram of brandy at Mrs. Hewlett's; and with the warmth of this did find myself in better order as to courage, truly. So we all up to the lobby; and between eleven and twelve o'clock were called in.

Pepys went on:

I began our defence most acceptably, and smoothly, and continued at it without any hesitation or losse . . . till half-past three in the afternoon, and so ended, without any interruption from the Speaker, but we withdrew. And there all my fellow-officers, and all the world that was within hearing, did congratulate me, and cry up my speech as the best thing they ever heard; and my fellow-officers were overjoyed in it.

On Monday 4 May 1668 the House reverted to the case of Peter Pett, and the final form of the articles of impeachment against him were approved. The introduction to these recited that the House 'do pray, that the said Peter Pett may be called to answer the said several Crimes and Misdemeanours, and receive such condign Punishment as the same shall deserve'.[1]

Pett had been formally dismissed as Commissioner of the Navy on 7 February 1668, and this had involved the loss of his official residence at Chatham, a 'mighty pretty house' as Pepys later described it in his diary on 26 March 1669. Pett's own private property was removed from the house, and he claimed that not all of it was restored to him. In a letter to Pepys on 25 June 1668 he wrote:

I have received some of my goods without interception, but my great dial, garden pots and figures, and marble table and 2 brewing vessels, which are as much my own as the coat on my back—as Lord Brouncker

---

[1] *Journals of the House of Commons*, Vol. IX, 1667–87, 4 May 1668.

can testify, having seen my books—were stopped by Captain Rand on order from Colonel Middleton.[1]

Pett's dismissal from office and the loss of his official residence proved in the end to be the only punishment meted out to him, for the articles of impeachment were not proceeded with. It was no doubt realized in high places that Pett could put up a good defence, and that in doing so he would incriminate with more or less good cause a number of prominent people. He was thus allowed to retire into obscurity, and four years afterwards, in 1672, he died quite unnoticed. By that date he had become a man forgotten, even by his former detractors.

[1] C.S.P.D., 1667–8, p. 459.

CHAPTER XI

Retrospect

IN VIEW OF the risks involved in the operation, the Dutch losses
in ships and men during the Medway raid were remarkably
slight. Their losses in ships amounted to only nine, or possibly
ten, fireships. Four of these were lost on Wednesday 12 June,
during the action at the chain in Gillingham Reach, and a further
five the following day in the attack on the ships at Upnor. Previously, during the engagement at Sheerness, another fireship
had been employed by the Dutch, and Edward Gregory, who
witnessed the action, stated in a letter to Pepys that this fireship
'burnt and drove into the harbour',[1] so it seems very probable
that it too was lost.

It is impossible to say with any accuracy what the Dutch losses
were in killed, wounded and captured. De Ruyter stated in his
log-book that the total Dutch losses during the operations on 12
and 13 June were 'only about thirty'; but other estimates vary
from fifty[2] to one hundred and fifty.[3] Even if the last figure is
accepted, it represents a very small loss in the light of what the
Dutch achieved. In the attack on Sheerness they suffered, it would
seem, no casualties at all. During the engagement at the chain,
too, their losses were not great, because of the poor opposition
which they encountered. Most of their casualties occurred during
the fierce cannonade on Thursday 13 June, when they attacked
the *Royal James*, *Royal Oak*, and *Loyal London* at Upnor; and the
losses they then sustained no doubt powerfully influenced their
decision to go no higher up the river, but to withdraw.

[1] Rawlinson MS. A. 195, f. 129.
[2] J. C. de Jonge, *Geschiedenis van het Nederlandsche Zeewesen*, Haarlem, 1859, Vol. II,
p. 200.
[3] M. A. de Wicquefort, *Histoire des Provinces Unies*, Amsterdam, 1866, Vol. III, p. 313.

The English loss in ships was not catastrophic, but serious and shameful in the light of the circumstances. The *Royal Charles* and *Unity* were captured by the Dutch; the *Royal James*, *Royal Oak*, and *Loyal London* burnt down to the water-line by them; the *Matthias*, *Charles V*, and *Sancta Maria* set on fire and destroyed. In addition to these losses the English themselves had sunk five fireships (*Dolphin*, *Barbados Merchant*, *Unicorn*, *John and Sarah*, *Constant John*); two ketches (*Edward and Eve*, *Hind*); and one dogger (*Fortune*) at the Mussel Bank in an endeavour to hinder the Dutch. The latter set fire to the upper works of these vessels during their withdrawal, so that they ultimately became a total loss. At the chain the English had sunk the *Marmaduke* and the *Norway Merchant*; and another smaller vessel there, a horse-boat called the *Prosperous* was burnt by the Dutch. At Sheerness the *Crown and Brill* had likewise been destroyed by the Dutch.

Apart from the above vessels which were lost, others were damaged or put temporarily out of action as a result of the decision taken on Wednesday 12 June to scuttle the men-of-war lying above Upnor lest the Dutch should continue their advance and capture or destroy them. Most of these ships were taken to the sides of the river and sunk in shallow water, but were afterwards (with one exception, the *Vanguard*) recovered and put into service again.

It is difficult to estimate the number of Englishmen killed, wounded and captured during the Medway action, since no exact totals seem to have been compiled or, at least, to have been preserved. Edward Gregory stated that one man had been killed and another wounded during the attack on Sheerness Fort, before the majority of the garrison fled; and it is probable that these were indeed the only casualties. During the action at the chain on Wednesday, when the Dutch met more opposition, there must have been a number of killed and wounded on the English side; and certainly prisoners were taken by the Dutch from the *Unity* and *Charles V*. It was probably during the engagement on Wednesday that most of the English casualties were sustained; for on Thursday, at Upnor, the main opposition to the Dutch came from Upnor Castle and the guns on the opposite shore of the river, and there is no mention of any casualties among the men serving the guns.

There is likewise no record of casualties on board the *Royal James*, *Royal Oak*, and *Loyal London*, with the exception of Captain Douglas. The inference is that the men detailed to defend these vessels must, like the garrison of Sheerness Fort, have deserted their posts. In the absence of precise figures it is difficult to make even a rough estimate of the English losses during the Medway action; but if the fifty to seventy prisoners which the Dutch claim to have taken are included, the total losses including killed and wounded may have been a hundred to a hundred and fifty. A correspondent of Lord Conway, on 15 June, stated that 'above 500 men' had been lost during the engagement in the Medway,[1] but he gave no authority for this figure, and it may have been a guess. Because of the general lack of opposition by the English at close quarters, the presumption must be that their losses during the fighting were well below five hundred.

One of the few redeeming features of the Medway disaster from the English point of view was the very slight loss of life, if not of property, sustained by civilians. None appears to have been killed on the Isle of Sheppey or at Gillingham, and although during the fierce engagement at Upnor on 13 June one civilian died, this was entirely accidental. He happened to be lying on a hill above Upnor watching the action when he was hit by a stray bullet which killed him.

Some two weeks after the Dutch raid, on 30 June 1667, Pepys visited Chatham Dockyard and was afterwards rowed down the river to Gillingham. In his diary that day he referred to the chivalrous conduct of the Dutch during their operations, and observed:

It seems very remarkable to me, and of great honour to the Dutch, that those of them that did go on shore to Gillingham, though they went in fear of their lives, and were some of them killed, and notwithstanding their provocation at Scelling [i.e. Terschelling], yet killed none of our people nor plundered their houses, but did take some things of easy carriage and left the rest, and not a house burned; and, which is to our eternal disgrace, that what my Lord Douglas's men, who

[1] C.S.P.D., 1667, pp. 189-90.

153

come after them, found there, they plundered and took all away: and the watermen that carried us did further tell us, that our own soldiers are far more terrible to those people of the country towns than the Dutch themselves.

One of the duties which devolved on Pepys as Clerk of the Acts was to ascertain, after the Dutch raid in the Medway, the total material loss which the State had sustained in regard to ships and stores. He wrote to James Norman, Clerk of the Survey at Chatham, for this information, and received in reply on 17 August 1667 a detailed account of the damage which had been done, and the financial loss which it represented.[1]

Norman said he would not try to estimate the value of the *Royal Charles*, *Royal James*, *Royal Oak*, and *Loyal London*, since he thought Pepys himself was in a better position to do this. However, Norman estimated various items on board those ships, such as cables and small cordage, which had been destroyed, at £1,000 at least. He considered that it would cost about £400 to repair the *Vanguard*, which had been scuttled by the dockyard officials; and he put the value of the *Dolphin*, *Constant John*, *Unicorn*, *John and Sarah*, and *Barbados Merchant*, sunk at the Mussel Bank, at £4,100, for in his view those vessels were probably 'utterly lost'. The *Hind*, *Edward and Eve*, and *Fortune*, sunk at the same place, he thought might be recovered, and he estimated the cost of repairs to them at £500.

He estimated the value of the *Unity*, captured by the Dutch, at £900, that of the *Matthias*, destroyed, at £800, and the *Charles V*, also destroyed, at £550. The *Marmaduke*, sunk by the English near to the chain, had, Norman declared, only just been refitted and was 'the best wreck in the river'; and so he put her value at £1,000. He estimated the value of the *Norway Merchant*, which had likewise been sunk by the English at the chain, even higher, at £1,400; for, he said, she had been fitted out and victualled for a voyage. He valued the *Sancta Maria*, burnt by the Dutch, at £600, the *Helverson* (*Hilversum*)[2] at £200 if she should be re-

---

[1] Rawlinson MS. A. 195, ff. 106–7.

[2] The *Helverson* (or *Helversome*) on her way to Sheerness on 22 July 1667 had run on to the stump of the mainmast of the *Norway Merchant* lying sunk off Gillingham by the chain, and being thus holed, the *Helverson* herself sank.

floated and repaired, but at £1,200 if she proved a total loss. Finally, Norman valued the *Prosperous*, a small boat used for transporting horses, which had been burnt near the chain, at £150.

He next considered the various ships which had been scuttled on Wednesday 12 June as a panic measure, and stated that though they were 'safe and well as to the main' they had nevertheless suffered damage to their upper works which he reckoned would cost £900 to repair.

Having dealt with the ships, Norman turned next to Sheerness Fort and Dockyard, where he estimated the total loss in buildings and stores at £3,000. The chain at Gillingham represented, in his view, a loss of £150, and its various appurtenances —a crane, stages, and cables run over it to strengthen it—which had been lost or destroyed, a further £400. Moreover, Norman said, a sum of £2,200 had been spent at Chatham in payment of wages to seamen and riggers and other men, purely as a consequence of the Dutch raid, and he himself had paid out £1,900 as compensation for loss of clothes, and to meet other contingencies arising from the raid. Lastly, he estimated that victuals to the value of £1,040 had been lost.

All together the sums enumerated by Norman amounted to nearly £22,000—but it must be remembered that he had not included the value of the *Royal Charles* and the three men-of-war burnt at Upnor. Nor did he (and he explicitly mentioned this) include in his valuation guns, powder, shot, and other material lost or destroyed, for which the Ordnance Commissioners were responsible. However, even if these omissions are borne in mind, it still remains a fact that the material damage suffered as a result of the Medway raid was relatively slight, when the magnitude of the operation is taken into account. If the Dutch had been able to continue their attack, and destroy or capture the remaining ships in the river, also to destroy the dockyard installations at Chatham, the story would, of course, have been different. But as it was, although the material loss sustained was certainly not negligible, it was not as important in its repercussions as the psychological effect of the English defeat on the morale of the nation.

Norman had estimated the cost of repairs to some of the sunken ships on the assumption that they might be successfully salvaged; but this expectation proved to be unduly optimistic. On 19 July the officials of Chatham Dockyard informed the Navy Board that in their opinion it would be worth while removing the *Royal James*, *Royal Oak*, and *Loyal London* to the Thames, there to be rebuilt. On 15 September the *Royal James* and *Loyal London* were accordingly taken into the Thames, and the former was put in dry-dock at Woolwich, the latter at Deptford. The estimate finally made of the cost of rebuilding the *Royal James* was £9,800, and this was considered unwarrantable, so that in April 1669 plans were being considered that the ship should be used as a hulk. She was spared this last indignity, however, and was broken up at Chatham in August 1670. The *Loyal London* fared better, was rebuilt, and launched at Deptford on 25 July 1670; but the *Royal Oak*, which had long since been written off as a total loss, was still laid up as a wreck in the Medway in May 1671.

The work of recovering the men-of-war which had been scuttled above Upnor was carried out successfully during the weeks following the Dutch withdrawal, and by the end of January 1668 all these wrecks had been cleared above Upnor, and at Gillingham the *Helverson* had been raised. The sunken ships lying further down the river and at the Mussel Bank presented, however, much greater difficulties. Yet it was absolutely necessary to clear them as soon as possible, for as long as they remained pilots refused to take ships up and down the Medway. On 5 April 1668 Colonel Thomas Middleton, Surveyor of the Navy at Chatham, wrote to Pepys from the dockyard and stated that the raising of the wrecks should be arranged on almost any terms, because the longer they remained the greater would be the damage to the navigation of the river. 'The work must be done,' he emphasized, 'or farewell in a short time to the Medway.'[1]

The Navy Board, impressed by the representations made by Middleton, took the matter in hand, and on 14 May 1668 an agreement was signed between the Board and Major Henry

[1] C.S.P.D., 1667–8, pp. 329–30.

Nicoll, by which the latter undertook to clear the Medway of the fourteen wrecks which were said to be still obstructing the navigation of the river. In return the Navy Board promised to lend Nicoll four vessels with all necessary appliances, and to pay him £300 down and a further £100 on completion of the work. In addition Nicoll was to have the right to sell such parts of the wrecks as he recovered, with the exception of guns, shot and anchors.

Nicoll was assisted by a partner named Edward Moorcock, of Chatham, but disputes soon arose between them, and other difficulties occurred which were caused, so Nicolls alleged, by the defects in equipment supplied by the Navy Board. On 18 July, therefore, Nicoll asked to be given more salvage vessels, more equipment and money, in default of which he asked to be released from his contract. His request was not granted, and so he withdrew from the work of salvage. This, however, was continued by Edward Moorcock with a new partner, John Moore. By February 1669 they had swept the river as far as the Mussel Bank and had recovered ten anchors, thirty-one guns, and other sunken objects. On 26 May they promised the Navy Board that they intended to proceed clearing the river 'with all expedition'; and in June 1669 they began work on the ships which had been sunk at the Mussel Bank. They found operations difficult, because the hulls had become filled with stiff clay and had settled about seven or eight feet into the the bed of the river. The work was heavy and exhausting, and Moorcock and Moore wrote to the Navy Board on 12 July asking for ten or twelve extra tuns of beer to be sent down. 'The number of men we are forced to employ,' they explained, 'expend the beer so fast this hot weather.'[1]

While the work of clearing the wrecks at the Mussel Bank was going on, attempts were made to lift the *Marmaduke*, which had been sunk near the chain in Gillingham Reach. The attempts failed, however, and on 3 September it was decided to offer her for sale, the buyer to have the task of removing or demolishing her. By this time three of the ships at the Mussel Bank had been removed, but since those remaining proved difficult, it was

---

[1] C.S.P.D., 1668–9, p. 406.

proposed to have them blown up to save further expense. It was also decided that other wrecks higher up the river, which it had not been possible to raise, were to be offered for sale like the *Marmaduke*, the buyers to be responsible for removing the wrecks, or for breaking them up.

On 2 October a group of dockyard officials including Phineas Pett, Edward Gregory, William Rand, and John Brooke inspected the wrecks still lying in the Medway, and made a valuation of them by order of Commissioner Cox. Their valuation, which Cox enclosed in a letter to the Navy Board on 4 October 1669, was as follows:

The bottom of the Dutch fireship above Upnor Castle..	£5 0s. 0d.
The bottom of the *Charles V*......................	£5 0s. 0d.
The bottom of the *Sancta Maria*....................	£12 0s. 0d.
The bottom of the bigger Dutch fireship at Gillingham..	£6 0s. 0d.
The bottom of the smaller Dutch fireship at Gillingham.	£4 0s. 0d.
The wreck of the Dutch fireship at Gillingham........	£15 0s. 0d.
The bottom of the *Barbados Merchant* at Hoo Creek.....	£3 0s. 0d.
The *Dolphin* at the Mussel Bank....................	£30 0s. 0d.
The dogger (*Fortune*) at the Mussel Bank.............	£10 0s. 0d.
The *John and Sarah* at the Mussel Bank...............	£23 0s. 0d.
The *Constant John*—not in a condition to be weighed....	– – –
	£113 0s. 0d.[1]

On 22 September 1669 the *Marmaduke* had been sold to a Mr. Gould for £151, and on 12 October the following wrecks were sold at public auction to him also:

The bottom of the Dutch fireship above Upnor Castle..	£7 0s. 0d.
The bottom of the *Charles V*......................	£8 0s. 0d.
The bottom of the bigger Dutch fireships at Gillingham.	£11 0s. 0d.
The bottom of the smaller Dutch fireship at Gillingham.	£7 0s. 0d.
The wreck of a Dutch fireship at Gillingham..........	£21 0s. 0d.
	£54 0s. 0d.

At the same public auction Richard Boys of London bought:

The bottom of the *Sancta Maria*....................	£21 0s. 0d.
The bottom of the *Barbados Merchant*................	£3 15s. 0d.
The wreck of the *Dolphin*..........................	£33 0s. 0d.

[1] S.P. 29 (266), f. 26.

The wreck of the *Fortune*.............................	£22 0s. 0d.
Thirty tons of rakings................................	£4 16s. 0d.
	£84 11s. 0d.

Finally, on the same date John Moore bought at the auction the *John and Sarah* for £30,[1] thus bringing the total realized by the sale to £168 11s. 0d., a sum well above the valuation of the dockyard officials. The higher prices realized were partly due to the fact that the purchasers hoped that with so much work going on in the river on the strengthening of fortifications, there would be a good chance of selling the planks and other timber obtained from the wrecks. But, as Commissioner Cox explained in a letter to the Navy Board on 20 October, there was another reason why the selling price exceeded the valuation. 'There would not have been so much given for them [i.e. the wrecks], he said, 'if we had not ordered some of the officers to be bidders.'[2]

The remaining wrecks which had not been sold, with the exception of the *Royal Oak* and *Defiance*, were finally destroyed by firing explosive charges in them during the last three months of 1669. On 3 January 1670 Commissioner Cox wrote to the Navy Board to inform them that he had terminated the contract of Moorcock and Moore and had discharged the men who had been employed in clearing the wrecks. These, he added, had all been blown to pieces, but two or three more chests of explosives would have to be used to clear the river completely.

Cox did not take into account the wrecks which had been bought by Gould and Boys, for these were not broken up till later, in 1670. It was not till May in that year, for example, that Gould began to break up the *Marmaduke*. Boys was even more dilatory, and Commissioner Cox had to write to the Navy Board suggesting that he should be ordered to come down forthwith to Chatham to supervise the breaking up of the wrecks which he had bought. Pressure by the Board had its effect, and by the end of 1670 the river was at last entirely clear again for navigation, and the few remaining marks of England's humiliation in June 1667 removed. The operations had, however, taken three years,

---

[1] Ibid., f. 84.   [2] C.S.P.D., 1668–9, p. 540.

despite the urgency involved, and the delay reveals the continuing inefficiency and sluggishness of the naval administration, despite the shock of the Medway disaster.

On 30 June 1667 Pepys travelled down to Chatham, and wrote later in his diary that he saw

the boats come up from Chatham with them that rowed with bandeleeres about their shoulders, and muskets in their boats; they being the workmen of the Yard, who have promised to redeem their credit, lost by their deserting the service when the Dutch were there.

The dockyardmen's effort to redeem themselves proved, however, short-lived, for soon they were complaining again about non-payment of their wages; and indeed all the traditional dockyard abuses—corruption, theft, absenteeism—began again as if the Medway disaster had never occurred. In July 1668 Phineas Pett, nephew of the disgraced Peter Pett, and Master-Shipwright at Chatham, was brought to book for dishonesty and embezzlement of government stores, and deprived of his office in September of that year. Despite his guilt and his bad reputation, Phineas was later reinstated, and proved thereafter to be a continuous source of trouble to Cox, the able and incorrupt commissioner of the dockyard. On 25 March 1671 Cox felt impelled to write to the Navy Board about Phineas Pett's idleness and untruthfulness; 'I despair,' he complained, 'of ever seeing things better looked after while he [i.e. Pett] continues master-shipwright.'[1] Despite all Commissioner Cox's representations Phineas Pett was not removed from his office, and the dockyard remained, as James Norman, Clerk of the Survey, had said in a letter of 23 September 1667 to Sir William Batten, 'miserably infected with thieves and pilfering rogues'.[2] Even after the shock of the Dutch raid in the Medway the Augean stables at Chatham remained uncleaned.

Though corruption and inefficiency in the dockyard had contributed towards the defeat, the major causes must be sought elsewhere. The most important, without doubt, was the lack of funds, for it was from this deficiency that most of the other evils

[1] C.S.P.D., 1671, p. 150.   [2] C.S.P.D., 1667, p. 478.

sprang. Equally, there can be no doubt that Parliament, and not Charles II, must be held responsible for the financial stringency. The Court and City circles who exerted a powerful influence at Westminster had willed the war, but did not provide the means with which it could be effectively waged. The revenues voted by Parliament were quite insufficient for the purpose, and there is little evidence to substantiate the traditional allegation that Charles II spent on his mistresses vast sums which had been voted for the upkeep of the Navy.

In 1667 a law was passed setting up a committee of the House of Commons to inquire into the spending of the sums which had been voted for the war. The report of the committee, submitted to the Commons in November 1669, revealed that an amount of £4,355,047 had been raised by additional votes, and that at least £4,335,244 of this had been duly spent on the war. The committee's report also revealed that Charles II had, as a desperate expedient, devoted the proceeds of customs, excise, hearth money, sale of prizes, and the sale of Dunkirk to the prosecution of the war, though they should normally have been used to finance the general administration of the country. It is true that the parliamentary committee was not satisfied with regard to a sum of £698,357 which the Earl of Anglesey, Treasurer of the Navy, had been responsible for, and there was doubt also with regard to another sum, amounting to £780,139, for which Anglesey's predecessor, Carteret, was held responsible. The committee was not, however, able to decide with certainty whether or not these sums had been devoted to other purposes than the war.[1]

Though the funds voted by Parliament for the war were insufficient, they amounted in all, nevertheless, to a large sum; and it is a matter of debate whether the money could have been better spent than it was, and the Medway disaster thereby mitigated, if not altogether averted. In this connection the decision that was taken not to fit out the customary large battle fleet for 1667 is open to criticism. Instead of sending out such a fleet a few small squadrons were kept in being in widely separated ports, to harass Dutch trade, and when the Dutch attacked in the Medway

[1] D. Ogg, *England in the Reign of Charles II*, Oxford, 1956, p. 318.

these squadrons were too far away to be of any use. If they had been kept together and stationed in or near the Thames Estuary, the course of events would undoubtedly have taken a different turn.

When the committee appointed by the House of Commons to inquire into the miscarriages of the war reported on 14 February 1668, it referred to the dispersal of the squadrons, and reported to the House as a miscarriage:

that notwithstanding His Majesty had eighteen thousand men in pay in dispersed ships in the year 1667, there was not a sufficient number of ships left to secure the rivers of Medway and Thames.[1]

On 22 February the House duly carried a resolution endorsing the committee's finding; but long before this the policy of dispersing the ships had come under vigorous attack in the country at large. As soon as the Medway defeat proved what a blunder had been made in not keeping a fleet in being at all costs, and in dispersing some ships and laying up others, mutual recriminations ensued within the king's immediate circle of advisers, and everybody sought to evade responsibility for the ill-fated decision by trying to put the blame on someone else.

According to one report[2] only the Duke of York, Prince Rupert, Albemarle, and the Archbishop of Canterbury had been against the laying-up of the men-of-war, and the majority of the Privy Council had persuaded Charles II against his will and own better judgement not to fit out a fleet. Other accounts accuse Sir William Coventry of having been the prime instigator of the mistaken policy. Evelyn wrote in his diary on 24 July 1667 that Coventry was one of those to blame for advising that the fleet should be laid up; and earlier Pepys had noted in his diary on 14 June that 'everywhere people do speak high against Sir W. Coventry', though he added that he believed Coventry was the best minister the king had. Pepys went on to record:

They say the Duke of Albemarle did tell my Lord Brouncker to his face that this discharging of the great ships there [i.e. at Chatham] was the cause of all this; and I am told that it is become common talk

[1] *Journals of the House of Commons*, Vol. IX, 1667–87, 14 February 1668.
[2] C.S.P.D., 1667, p. xxiv.

against my Lord Brouncker. But in that he is to be justified, for he did it by verbal order from Sir W. Coventry, and with good intent; and it was to good purpose, whatever the success be, for the men would have but spent the King so much the more in wages, and yet not attended on board to have done the King any service.

Apart from the fact that he was ill served with advice from his ministers, Charles II was also put at a disadvantage because of faulty intelligence, or because intelligence reports were not heeded. During the secret negotiations with Louis XIV at the end of 1666 and the beginning of 1667 the complacent and over-optimistic reports of Lord St. Albans induced Charles to place too much reliance on the good faith of the French king as a mediator with the Dutch. St. Albans's reports led Charles to believe that peace was as good as concluded, and this undoubtedly influenced him in deciding to lay up the battle-fleet. Equally serious in its effects was the negligence of Lord Arlington to take proper notice of the communications which were reaching his secretary Joseph Williamson from the Netherlands during the spring of 1667. These gave detailed information about the strength and movements of the Dutch fleet, and from them a clear deduction could be drawn that the Dutch were preparing for an offensive operation of considerable importance. Nevertheless, no such deduction seems to have been drawn by Arlington or other members of the Council; or, if they did read anything into the reports reaching Williamson, they took no action to ensure that all possible preparations were made to meet an attack, with the speed and thoroughness which the situation, as revealed by the reports, called for.

Afterwards, when the search for scapegoats was in progress, Arlington seems to have realized that his failure correctly to interpret the intelligence reports which had been brought to his notice could justly be accounted a contributory cause of the Medway disaster. His ignoble reaction was to hope that if Peter Pett could be offered up as a sacrifice to the clamour of the populace for revenge and punishment, he himself and other members of the Government might escape retribution. In a letter to the Duke of Ormonde on 18 June 1667 he stated, quite frankly,

'If he [i.e Peter Pett] deserve hanging, as most thinke he does, and have it, much of the staine will be wip'd off of the Government which lyes heavily upon it.'[1]

Even if it is assumed that in the prevailing circumstances the Dutch raid in the Medway could not have been altogether prevented, it is still arguable that some of its worst consequences could have been avoided or lessened had certain measures been taken in good time. In the first place, if Sheerness Fort had been completed and strongly garrisoned by the time the Dutch arrived at the Nore in June 1667, there can be little doubt that the Medway raid would have taken a very different course from what it actually did. If the Dutch had been unable to take the fort, it is unlikely that they would have ventured up the Medway. Prince Rupert, in the narrative which he submitted to the House of Commons, took this view:

Though many months passed before the Dutch made their attempt yet nothing had been done to render Sheerenesse defensible against an enemy: to which neglect we may justly ascribe the burning of the ships at Chatham and the dishonour that attended it.[2]

The committee appointed by the House of Commons to inquire into the miscarriages of the war later endorsed Prince Rupert's view, and reported on 14 February 1668:

It is the humble opinion of this committee that the firing of His Majesty's ships in the River of Medway, to the great dishonour of the nation, was chiefly occasioned by the neglect of finishing the fort at Sheerenesse.[3]

From the details supplied by the committee it appears that the Ordnance Commissioners were responsible for the failure to complete the fort in good time. They had been ordered by the Duke of York on 23 March 1667 to construct the fort, but it was not till 27 April that the Commissioners had sent Captain Valentine Price to Sheerness to supervise the construction. Moreover, from then until the appearance of the Dutch in the Thames Estuary, work on the construction of the defences had been

[1] V. Barbour, *Henry Bennet, Earl of Arlington*, London, 1914, p. 109.
[2] *Journals of the House of Commons*, Vol. IX, 1667–87, 31 October 1667.
[3] Ibid., 14 February 1668.

carried on in dilatory fashion partly owing to shortage of work-men, so that the fort was still uncompleted when the Dutch arrived.

After they had taken Sheerness Fort, the Dutch might still have been hindered sufficiently at the Mussel Bank to deter them from attempting to sail higher up the river. Though the vessels sunk there did not block the channel completely, they caused sufficient of an obstruction to force the Dutch to move at least one of them (the ketch *Edward and Eve*) to give the larger vessels of van Ghent's squadron unimpeded passage. If one or two more ships had been sunk by the English at the Mussel Bank, and if men and guns had been sent to cover the river passage there, to hinder the Dutch from moving the sunken ships, the advance might have been considerably delayed, if not stopped com-pletely.

Finally, when the Dutch reached the chain at Gillingham, their further progress might have been prevented if the *Sancta Maria* had been sunk in the fairway between the *Marmaduke* and the *Norway Merchant*. Albemarle, in his narrative presented to the House of Commons, was emphatic on this point:

If that ship [i.e. the *Sancta Maria*] had been sunk in the place where I had appointed, the Dutch ships could not have got beyond those of ours sunk within the chain, and thereby none of the King's ships, within, could have been destroyed.[1]

According to Albemarle the *Sancta Maria* had been run aground in Cockham Wood Reach because of the carelessness of the pilot and the two Masters of Attendance of Chatham Dockyard, who were also on board. Some years later, in December 1671, Phineas Pett placed the blame solely on Captain John Brooke, one of the Masters of Attendance, and alleged that he had run the *Sancta Maria* aground through laziness and neglect to make the best use of the tide. At the time when he wrote, Phineas was engaged in a dispute with Captain Brooke, and he may therefore have made his allegation from spite. No proceedings were ever taken against Brooke, so that whether he ran the *Sancta Maria* aground through

[1] Ibid., 31 October 1667.

negligence, or whether it was a pure accident, remains an open question.

It was not Brooke, however, but Peter Pett against whom the most serious charges were made in connection with the Medway disaster, and it is instructive to examine these one by one, as they were listed in the articles of impeachment drawn up against him, to see how far they can be substantiated. After Pett was released on bail he prepared an answer to the various charges, and what appears to be a version of this is preserved in the British Museum.[1] This document, which is unsigned, is entitled: 'The Case of Peter Pett Esqr One of the Com^{rs} of his Maj^{tys} Navy'.

It rebuts charges that Pett had been negligent in not advising that a fort should be built at Sheerness; in not fitting out ships in the spring of 1667; in not having the large men-of-war taken higher up the Medway in furtherance of the Duke of York's order; in not having the long-boats and pinnaces built and equipped which the Duke of York had also ordered; lastly, in misemploying some of the boats to carry away Pett's own personal property.

In rebuttal it was said that Pett had frequently advised that a fort should be built at Sheerness, that he had done all in his power to have ships properly fitted out, and that he had issued orders to have the large men-of-war carried higher up the river. As for the long-boats and pinnaces, these, it was said, had been built and fitted out in good time under Pett's supervision. With regard to the use of boats to transport his personal belongings, it was admitted that Pett had used the *James* yacht and a pinnace to take to a place of safety his plans and models of ships, dockyard records, and seamen's tickets worth several thousand pounds. Moreover, it was affirmed, the two boats had been used for the purpose at a time when there had been no other demand for them, so that their employment had done no harm.

Articles I to III of the impeachment accused Pett of having failed to move the larger men-of-war, and particularly the *Royal Charles*, higher up the Medway; and Peter Pett's reply to this charge cannot be said to be convincing. He had received orders

[1] Harleian MS. 7018, f. 92.

as early as March to move the ships; but when the Dutch appeared some of the vessels had still not been carried higher up the river. It was no defence to claim, as Pett did, that he had in fact issued orders to have the *Royal Charles* moved. It was his duty, as Commissioner, to see that the orders were carried out, and this he signally failed to do. It is true that Pett very tardily, on Tuesday morning 11 June, had given instructions that the *Royal Charles* should be towed higher up the river; but the men he ordered to do this had no sooner boarded her than they were told (by whom is not known) to transport soldiers who were on board to Gillingham—and so the *Royal Charles* remained at her moorings.[1]

Article V of the impeachment alleged that Pett had been so negligent in his duties that although he had eight hundred men under him at Chatham only ten had reported for duty when the Dutch sailed up the Medway. This accusation (which was not mentioned in 'The Case of Peter Pett') was palpably absurd. The men absented themselves from duty because of their complete lack of morale; but this could not be ascribed to Pett. It was due to the general maladministration of the Navy and, particularly, to the non-payment of wages.

Articles VI and VII accused Pett of having refused to supply a sufficient number of tools for the construction of batteries, and of having supplied deal planks instead of oaken planks for the gun platforms. The indictment alleged that he had not issued all the tools which were available, and that he had not provided oaken planks although there had been 'several oaken planks' available in the Yard. It is impossible to ascertain whether any significant quantity of tools remained unused in store owing to Pett's orders, or negligence; but it is certain that the shortage of plank-wood cannot be ascribed to him. During the spring of 1667 Pett had written several times to the Navy Board, complaining about the lack of timber and plank in the dockyard; and there was in fact such a shortage at the time of the Medway emergency that the wooden floor of the ropeyard had to be ripped up so that the planks could be used to make gun platforms.

Article IV of the original draft indictment, which had accused

Pett of misemploying boats for the transport of personal belongings, was omitted from the final approved draft of the articles of
impeachment, and with good cause. In October 1667 fourteen
boatswains and eleven shipwrights who had had charge of the
long-boats and pinnaces during the Medway raid were required
by the Navy Board to answer a number of questions about their
activities at that time. The seventh and last of these questions
was: 'The times that your boat, or any boat, was employed in
carrying of goods from the yard or town, whose they were, and
by whose order.'[1]

It is significant that most of the men in command of boats
denied having any knowledge of how other boats had been employed, because, so they said, they themselves had been kept fully
occupied in carrying out their own duties. Other men specifically
denied that their boats had been used to carry goods, and they
said that to the best of their knowledge no other boats had been
so employed. One of the boat commanders, however, a shipwright
named Leonard Collard, did testify that on Thursday 13 June
he had been told by Phineas Pett to report to Commissioner
Peter Pett's house; Collard's statement continued:

When I came to the door the Commr. ordered mee to goe up and
breake open a closett to take out his writeings, and then to carry them
down to the waterside, and when I came there he asked the builder
[i.e. the Master Shipwright, Phineas Pett, the Commissioner's nephew]
what I was, but his answer I know not. And then he ordered mee to
putt them into the boate, being about eleaven of the clock, and to
carry them up above bridge [i.e. Rochester Bridge], and delivered
them aboard of the *Jemmie* [i.e. the *James* yacht], and then I came downe
on Thursday night.[2]

A postscript added to Collard's evidence, written in another
hand, stated:

Hee saies that when he came above Rochester Bridge he saw severall
boates with goods in them, but whose goods they were he knowes not,
only at his returne he acquainted ye Comr with it, and thereupon by
order from my Ld Brouncker and ye Comr he and Goodman Wall
were employed to fetch downe these boates, which he accordingly did,
and gave my Lord an accompt thereof, and of the names of what men

[1] S.P. 46 (136), f. 584.   [2] Ibid., f. 606.

he found in ye boates wch were but few, for where ye goods were out ye men run away from ye boats when they saw him comeing.[1]

It is clear from Collard's evidence that Peter Pett did indeed send some of his 'writings', i.e. his ship designs and other dock-yard records further up the river into safety. These documents were not his household goods, but State property, and it can be argued that he did right to put them out of the enemy's reach. From the testimony of the boatswains and shipwrights it is equally clear that the pinnaces and long-boats which Pett had made ready in conformity with the Duke of York's instructions were properly employed during the action in the Medway, and that with the exception of Collard's boat, they had not been used to take goods higher up the Medway. The boats which Collard found above Rochester Bridge were other boats, and whether they were dockyard boats or privately owned is not known.

The general conclusion must be that although Peter Pett did not distinguish himself during the Medway action, his sins of omission and commission did not justify his being singled out for punishment whilst others went scot-free. On the other hand, however, it is obvious that he was a weak man. The portrait of him by Lely in the National Maritime Museum shows this, and Pett's despairing and pathetic appeals for help in the two letters which he sent to the Navy Board on 10 June are those of a man who lacked self-confidence and the capacity to control subordin-ates and direct affairs in an emergency.

Even if Pett had been superhuman, however, he would still have been daunted by the sheer lack of men and material, and the chaos and confusion, which prevailed at Chatham while the Dutch were in the Medway. Each of the long-boats and pinnaces which Pett had managed to fit out had a crew, which in some cases numbered as many as fourteen men; but none of these were given arms, though they naturally asked for them. The stark fact was, as Pett informed the commanders of the boats, that no arms were available.

Though there was a lamentable lack of material, there was no lack of direction from above during the Medway invasion. In

[1] Ibid., f. 606.

addition to Albemarle, Lord Brouncker, Lord Middleton, Lord Douglas, Sir John Mennes, and Sir Edward Spragge moved around during the emergency giving orders and counter-orders; and as if this plethora of command were not enough, Peter Pett, Phineas Pett and the two Masters of Attendance of Chatham Dockyard also issued instructions. Inevitably, men were ordered to do one thing only to be told shortly afterwards by someone else in authority to go elsewhere to do other work. This led to confusion, waste of time, and above all a further weakening of morale.

Albemarle, the supreme commander at Chatham, did all that was possible in the circumstances, but he was gravely handicapped by his lack of local knowledge, which left him dependent on advice from Peter Pett and other dockyard officials, who appear sometimes to have misled him. After he arrived at Chatham he stated optimistically in a letter sent to London that all the large ships in the Medway were secure, that he was very confident that the Dutch could do no harm there because of the chain and because of the ships which had been sunk to obstruct the channel. He was in fact so confident that he rashly rescinded a previous request made by himself that a thousand additional troops be sent to Chatham.

Sir William Coventry later read Albemarle's letter to the committee of the House of Commons which was inquiring into the miscarriages of the war; but this did not prejudice the committee against the Duke, and on 23 October 1667 the House of Commons passed a vote of thanks to him and Prince Rupert for their services. Pepys recorded in his diary that day that he thought this 'a strange act'; 'but', he went on, 'I know not how, the blockhead Albermarle hath strange luck to be loved, though he be (and every man must know it) the heaviest man in the world, but stout and honest to his country'.

From the Dutch point of view the most interesting question arising from the Medway expedition is whether they exploited their initial victories as fully as possible, or whether they might have done even better than they did. Many English accounts of the action took the view that the Dutch had missed a great chance by withdrawing down the Medway after the victorious engagement at Upnor on Thursday 13 June. For example, Clarendon wrote:

Without doubt, if the Dutch had prosecuted the present advantage they had, with the circumspection and courage that was necessary, they might have fired the Royal Navy at Chatham, and taken or destroyed all the ships which lay higher in the river, and so fully revenged themselves for what they had suffered at the Flie.[1]

In a letter to Pepys dated 20 July 1667 Edward Gregory at Chatham took the same view. After recounting the Dutch successes up to Wednesday 12 June, he said:

Having thus lost all that wch wee put o^r trust in, our fort, o^r fireships, o^r chaine, and guard-ships, the rest lay exposed to the enemies mercy, who had he had courage to have prosecuted his designe that tide, had undeniably have destroyed all the ships the Kinge is master of in this river; butt I suppose his acquisition of such a victory and soe great a prize [i.e. the *Royal Charles*] glutted and overjoyed him.[2]

There can be no doubt that Johan de Witt was disappointed that the Dutch forces had withdrawn on Friday 14 June without having attempted further attacks on the dockyard at Chatham and the ships lying higher up the Medway. In a letter to his brother Cornelis written on 20 June in reply to a communication of 13 June wherein Cornelis had explained why the decision had been taken to venture no further, Johan expressed great disappointment. It must not be said, he wrote in conclusion, '*vincere scit, victoriam uti nescit*' ('he knows how to win a victory, but not how to exploit it').

Some modern Dutch writers have echoed Johan de Witt's sentiments. Notably F. Muller van Brakel, in an article in the Dutch Navy periodical *Marineblad*, entitled 'The Expedition to Chatham only Half Successful',[3] has argued that it would have been well worth the risk to have continued the Dutch attack above Upnor. It is natural for Dutchmen to criticize the decision not to proceed

---

[1] *The Life of Edward Earl of Clarendon . . . Written by Himself*, Oxford, 1759, p. 421.
[2] Rawlinson MS. A. 195, f. 131.
[3] '*De Tocht naar Chatham slechts half geslaagd*'. *Marineblad*, Den Helder, February 1952, pp. 761–93.

any further; but in the light of the prevailing circumstances there can be little doubt that it was right. With each stage of the operation the English opposition had stiffened. The capture of Sheerness Fort had been effected without loss of Dutch lives: the attack on the chain had, however, met with more resistance; and on Thursday 13 June the fire from Upnor Castle and the guns on the opposite shore of the river inflicted many more casualties among the Dutch than they had previously sustained. They now found themselves high up a tortuous river, away from their main fleet at the mouth of the Thames. Their further passage up the Medway would be hindered by the increasing narrowness of the navigable channel and by sunken ships. Moreover the capacity of the English to hit back was manifestly improving, and the Dutch could not be certain about the strength of reinforcements which were on the way to, or had already arrived at Chatham. In such circumstances it was clearly prudent to rest content with what had already been achieved, and not to take risks which might have resulted in disaster.

What had already been achieved constituted indeed a memorable feat of arms. Fortuitous factors such as favourable winds and tides had no doubt helped the Dutch; but their victory was essentially due to their own naval skill and daring. The *Tocht naar Chatham*, as the operation is called by them, is an example of what men can do in face of formidable obstacles if they are brave and well led. It also remains an imperishable reminder of the qualities which raised the Dutch to the forefront of the nations in the seventeenth century, and which have sustained them ever since, in all vicissitudes.

Postscript

In 1967, the tercentary of the Medway raid, the English (one might almost say typically) commemorated this notorious naval defeat which they had suffered. In June a 'River Medway Dutch Week' was held, and of course the Dutch were invited to attend, which they did with alacrity and entirely without inhibitions. Racing and social events were arranged for the many Dutch visitors, some of whom arrived in their yachts in this second but peaceful invasion of the Medway. The Dutch Navy also sent over three vessels, while the Royal Navy was represented by the destroyer *Carysfort* which berthed amicably alongside the Dutch *Holland*.

The Dutch Press reacted goodhumouredly to what must have seemed a singular manifestation of the traditional English capacity to be good losers. The *Algemeen Handelsblad* in its issue of 2 June 1967 published a short article on the forthcoming week, but at the same time thought it necessary to inform its readers that the Medway was a tributary of the Thames, and that the town of Chatham was situated on it.

The Dutch ambassador, in a message to the people of the Medway Towns, declared that it was a source of real satisfaction to know that three hundred years after a Dutch naval force had invaded the River Medway, an initiative had been taken along the banks of the same river to commemorate the event. Not to be outdone in the exchange of civilities, the *Kent Messenger*, in its issue of 9 June 1967, said: 'To our Dutch friends the *Kent Messenger* extends this greeting: *Welkom in Kent. Wij hopen, dat U een prettige tijd heeft, en veel vrienden zult maken.*'[1]

This hope was realized, for during the week the Dutch visitors were treated to what was almost a surfeit of exhibitions and displays,

[1] 'Welcome to Kent. We hope that you will have a nice time, and make many friends.'

sailing races, and dances. On Saturday 10 June a contingent of Dutch sailors, dressed in seventeenth-century costume, marched to Queenborough Guildhall, where the Dutch flag was hoisted by the captain of the *Holland*. On Sunday 11 June the Dutch frigate *Fret* sailed up the Medway from Sheerness, escorted by yachts and other small craft, and *en route* passed through a curtain of coloured water put up by fire-fighting tugs. This watery barrier was meant to symbolize the chain, which had stretched across the river a few hundred yards below the point, off Admiralty Pier, Gillingham, where the *Fret* anchored. Here Mr. F. P. J. de Ruyter de Wildt, a descendant of Admiral de Ruyter, stepped ashore, to be welcomed by Councillor Harris, the Mayor of Gillingham, and by Captain Peter Petts, a descendant of Commissioner Peter Pett.

On Monday the band of the Royal Netherlands Marines played at Upnor Castle before an admiring crowd estimated at three thousand; and the inhabitants of Upnor declared later that there had not been so many visitors to the village within living memory. On Tuesday 13 June the Dutch band led a naval march through the streets of Chatham, and repeated this through the streets of Gillingham on Wednesday. During the evening Anglo-Dutch amity was further cemented when a ceremony was held at Queenborough and that ancient town was twinned with Brielle. On Saturday 17 June the band of H.M. Royal Marines beat retreat near Chatham Town Hall, and in the evening the Dutch flag was lowered from Queenborough Guildhall, and with these two ceremonies, apart from a few final events on Sunday, the River Medway Dutch Week came to an end.

The *Kent Messenger* had claimed, in its issue of 9 June 1967: The River Medway Dutch Week is a classic example of the urge to knit tighter the threads of commerce, goodwill, and community interchange with our cross-Channel relations'; and the *Chatham, Rochester and Gillingham News*, in its issue of 16 June, whose front page was decorated with a broad strip of the red, white, and blue of the Dutch colours, reported that with two days still to go the Dutch week had already proved to be 'a fantastic success', and that the goodwill which had been generated would almost certainly give rise to further similar ventures in the future. Ties which had been made between ordinary individuals were so strong that some of the Dutch visitors, it was said, were already talking about organizing their own equivalent of the Medway Week in Holland, in the near future.

It may well be that among these enthusiasts were some who had reached the conclusion that the commercial opportunities fostered by such a week were by no means negligible. This thought had evidently already occurred to some enterprising citizens of the Medway Towns, for at a reception on 14 June Councillor Foster was reported by the *Chatham, Rochester and Gillingham News* (16 June 1967) to have said that it was not strictly true to call the Medway Week a celebration. He added:

The Dutch might be celebrating it but as far as we are concerned it is more a commemoration, and one of the principal reasons why it is being held is to publicise the excellent port facilities in the Medway.

On this prosaic note it will perhaps be fitting to end, since Anglo-Dutch commercial rivalry in the seventeenth century had been one of the major causes of the hostilities which brought the Medway raid in their train.

Sources

(A) MANUSCRIPT

ALGEMEEN RIJKSARCHIEF (The Hague)

Eerste Afdeeling, Staten-Generaal

9248   Instruction to N. Ravens, Rotterdam, to visit Dutch prisons to try to persuade imprisoned English seamen to enter Dutch service

9336   Log-book of Lt.-Admiral Aert Jansz. van Nes.

Eerste Afdeeling, Collectie de Ruyter

17   Log-book of de Ruyter

Derde Afdeeling, Staten van Holland (1572–1795)

2707/4   Letters of Cornelis de Witt

BODLEIAN LIBRARY (Oxford)

Carte Papers

Vol. 35   Letters dated 11 and 15 June 1667 about events at Chatham (folios 474, 478)

Vol. 223   Letter dated 7 November 1667 relating to Peter Pett's examination by the House of Commons (folio 323)

Rawlinson MSS.

A. 195   Folio volume entitled 'Pepys Papers', containing correspondence with Pepys and other material relating to naval affairs.

D. 924   Account of the Dutch War from October 1666 to August 1667 (folios 227–36)

BRITISH MUSEUM

Additional MSS.

9314   Abstract of Navy Orders 1660–1700

11,684   Gibson's Collections on Naval Affairs.
         The Dutch Action at Chatham Examined (folios 31–3)

32,094   Reports of Albemarle and Prince Rupert to the House of
         Commons on the miscarriages of the Dutch War

33,413   Diary of J. Millward, M.P., 1666–8

Harleian MSS.

7018   Papers relating to the Army and Navy
       The Case of Peter Pett Examined (folio 92)

7170   Proceedings in Parliament and Papers Relating thereto
       1667–80

Sloane MSS.

655   Poetical Pieces of the Time of Charles II
      The Loyal Scott (folio 18)

2448   A Survey of the Medway from Rochester Bridge to Sheer-
       ness made 10–11 October 1667 (folios 39–40)

5222(5)   A New and Exact Survey of Rochester, Chatham and the
          River Medway . . . taken by Joseph Spice

Stowe MSS.

142   Letter of Charles II to Sir George Downing 16 January 1672

NATIONAL MARITIME MUSEUM (Greenwich)

MS. AGC/G1   Letter describing the Dutch attack in the Medway,
                13 June 1667

MS. WYN/15/1   Consultation held at Sheerness on 20 March 1667 to
                 devise means of making the Medway safe from
                 attack

MS. LBK/8   S. Pepys's Official Correspondence

MS. SER/78   Sergison Papers (Letters and other material relating
            to naval affairs)

PUBLIC RECORD OFFICE

S.P. 29 (State Papers Domestic, Charles II, 1668–9)

Vol. 240   Account of wrecks in the Medway
Vol. 265   Account of wrecks in the Medway
Vol. 266   Account of wrecks in the Medway

S.P. 46 (*State Papers Domestic—Supplementary*)

Vol. 136   Admiralty Papers 1660–73
Vol. 137   Admiralty Papers 1661–73

S.P. 84 (*State Papers Foreign—Holland*)

Vol. 182   January–June 1667
Vol. 183   July 1667–May 1668

(B) PRINTED

A Brief Character of the Low Countries under the States (London, 1652)

An Exact Survey of the Affaires of the United Netherlands (London, 1665)

Aitzema, Lieuwe van, *Saken van Staet en Oorlogh in ende omtrent de Vereenigde Nederlanden, beginnende met het Jaer 1667 ende eyndigende met het begin van't Jaer 1669* (Seste Deel) (The Hague, 1672)

Akveld, L. M. and Bruijn, J. R., 'Een Ooggetuige over Chatham' (in *Spiegel Historiael*, Bussum, June 1967)

Alle de Gedichten van J. Antonides van der Goes (Rotterdam, 1735)

Anderson, R. C., 'Dutch Flag Officers in 1665–67 and 1672–73' (in *Mariner's Mirror*, Vol. XXIV, No. 1, January 1938)

A Seasonable Expostulation with the Netherlands, Declaring their Ingratitude to, and the Necessity of their Agreement with, the Commonwealth of England (London, 1652)

Archaeologia Cantiana

Barbour, V., *Henry Bennet, Earl of Arlington* (London, 1914)

Baron van Heeckeren, C. A. L. H., 'Tocht van de Ruyter naar de Theems' (in *Kroniek van het Historisch Genootschap Gevestigd te Utrecht*, Zesde Serie, Vijfde Deel, Utrecht, 1875)

Basnage, M., *Annales des Provinces Unies* (2 vols., The Hague, 1726)

Bebington, T., *The Right Honourable the Earl of Arlington's Letters to Sir W. Temple* (London, 1701)

Beresford, J., *The Godfather of Downing Street: Sir George Downing 1623–1684* (London, 1925)

Blok, P., *The Life of Admiral de Ruyter* (trans. G. J. Renier, London, 1933)

Boxer, C. R., *The Dutch Seaborne Empire 1600–1800* (London, 1965)

Brandt, G., *La Vie de Michel de Ruiter* (Amsterdam, 1698)

British Museum *Catalogue of Prints and Drawings*, Div. I, *Political and Personal Satires* (London, 1870)

— Luttrell Collection, *Proclamations and Broadsides* (Vol. III)

Bryant, A., *King Charles II* (London, 1955)

— *Samuel Pepys: The Man in the Making* (London, 1947)

Burchett, J., *A Complete History of the Most Remarkable Transactions at Sea* (London, 1720)

Burnet, T., *Bishop Burnet's History of His Own Time* (Vol. I, London, 1809)

Calendar of State Papers Domestic (C.S.P.D.), 1645–73.

Calendar of Treasury Books, 1660–7, 1689–92.

Callender, G., *The Naval Side of British History* (London, 1940)

— *The Portrait of Peter Pett and the Sovereign of the Seas* (Newport, Isle of Wight, 1930)

Castlemaine, Earl of, *A Short and True Account of the Material Passages in the First War between the English and Dutch since His Majesties Restauration* (London, 1672)

Catalogus: Tentoonstelling ter herdenking van Michiel de Ruyter (Rijksmuseum, Amsterdam, 1957)

Chappell, E., *Shorthand Letters of Samuel Pepys* (Cambridge, 1933)

Charnock, J., *Biographia Navalis* (Vol. I, London, 1794)

Clarendon, Earl of, *The Life of Edward Earl of Clarendon, . . . Written by Himself* (Oxford, 1759)

Clark, G. N., *The Later Stuarts 1660–1714* (Oxford, 1965)

Clowes, W. L., *The Royal Navy: A History* (Vol. II, London, 1898)

Coleman, D. C., 'Naval Dockyards under the Later Stuarts' (in *Economic History Review*, Second Series, Vol. VI, No. 2, December 1953)

Colenbrander, H. T., *Bescheiden uit Vreemde Archieven omtrent de Groote Nederlandsche Zeeoorlogen 1652–76* (2 vols., The Hague, 1919)

Coles Finch, W., *The Medway River and Valley* (London, 1929)

Copland, J., *The Taking of Sheerness by the Dutch* (Sheerness, 1895)

Crofton, D. A., 'The Dutch in the Medway, June 9–13, 1667' (in *Journal of the Royal United Service Institution*, Vol. XXIX, London, 1885–6)

Cruden, R. P., *The History of the Town of Gravesend* (London, 1848)

Daly, A. A., *The History of the Isle of Sheppey* (London, 1904)

Davies, C. M., *The History of Holland and the Dutch Nation* (Vol. III, London, 1857)

Davies, K. G., *The Royal African Company* (London, 1957)

De Jonge, J. C., *Geschiedenis van het Nederlandsche Zeewesen* (Tweede Deel, Haarlem, 1859)

De Vries, T., *Tocht naar Chatham: Eeuwfeest voor een Nederlag* (Amsterdam, 1967)

De Vaynes, J. H. L., *The Kentish Garland* (Vol. I, Hertford, 1882)

De Wicquefort, M. A., *Histoire des provinces unies* (Vol. III, Amsterdam, 1866)

Dictionary of National Biography

Diekerhoff, F. L., *De Oorlogsvloot in de Zeventiende Eeuw* (Bussum, 1967)

Elias, J. E., *De Tweede Engelsche Oorlog als het Keerpunt in onze Betrekkingen met Engeland* (Amsterdam, 1930)

Edmundson, G., *Anglo-Dutch Rivalry during the First Half of the Seventeenth Century* (Oxford, 1911)

Evelyn, J., *Diary* (ed. E. S. De Beer, London, 1959)

Farnham Burke, H., 'The Builders of the Navy: A Genealogy of the Family of Pett' (in *The Ancestor*, No. X, July 1904)

Feiling, K., *British Foreign Policy 1660–72* (London, 1930)

Firth, C. H., *The Memoirs of Edmund Ludlow 1625–72* (Vol. II, Oxford, 1894)

— *A Commentary on Macaulay's History of England* (London, 1964)

Fisher, H. A. L., *A History of Europe* (London, 1938)

Fruin, R., and Japikse, N., *Brieven van Johan de Witt* (Derde Deel, 1665–9, Amsterdam, 1912)

Fulton, T. W., *The Sovereignty of the Sea* (Edinburgh and London, 1911)

Geddes, J., *History of the Administration of John de Witt* (London, 1879)

Geyl, P., *Oranje en Stuart 1641–72* (Arnhem, 1963)

— *The Netherlands in the Seventeenth Century: Part II, 1648–1715* (London, 1964)

— '*Stukken Betrekking Hebbende op den Tocht naar Chatham en Berustende op het Record Office te Londen*' (in *Bijdragen en Mededelingen van het Historisch Genootschap* (Utrecht), Deel 38, Amsterdam, 1917)

Griffith Davies, J. D., *Honest George Monck* (London, 1936)

Gumble, T., *The Life of General Monck, Duke of Albemarle* (London, 1671)

Haines Jones, N., 'Medway Landmarks' (in *The Blue Peter*, July 1938)

— 'The Dutch Attack in the Medway' (in *The Blue Peter*, November 1938)

Haley, K. D. H., *William of Orange and the English Opposition 1672–4* (Oxford, 1953)

Hartmann, C. H., *The King My Brother* (London, 1954)

Historical MSS. Commission
  MSS. of the Corporation of Trinity House (London, 1881)
  MSS. of the Duke of Portland, Vol. I, II (London, 1891 and 1893)
  MSS. of J. E. Hodgkin (London, 1897)
  MSS. of S. H. Le Fleming (London, 1890)
  MSS. of Earl Cowper (London, 1888)
Hollandsche Mercurius (Amsterdam, 1668)
Hollond, J., *Two Discourses of the Navy* (Navy Records Society, London, 1896)
Howarth, R. G., *Letters and the Second Diary of Samuel Pepys* (London, 1932)
James, Duke of York, *Memoirs of the English Affairs, Chiefly Naval, from the Year 1660 to 1673* (London, 1729)
James, H. A., *The Dutch in the Medway 1667* (Chatham, 1967)
Japikse, N., *Johan de Witt* (Amsterdam, 1918)
Joachim Oudaans Poëzy (Amsterdam, 1712)
Jones, D., *Letters Written by Sir William Temple During His Being Ambassador at The Hague to the Earl of Arlington and Sir John Trevor, Secretaries of State to King Charles II* (London, 1699)
Joyfull News for England, or, a Congratulatory Verse upon our late happy Success in Firing 150 Dutch Ships in their own Harbours (London, 1666)
Journals of the House of Commons, Vol. VIII (1660–7); Vol. IX (1667–87)
Journals of the House of Lords, Vol. XII (1666–75)
Kaerte van de Rivieren van London en Rochester of Chetham; waer in duydelick wert vertoont, op wat Plaetsen d'Oorloghs Vloot van hare Hoogh Mogende de Heeren Staten Generael der Vereenighde Nederlanden (door Godts zegen) wonderlick heeft vernielt en verovert de voornaemste Oorloghs Schepen van sijne Majesteyt van Groot Britannien (Amsterdam, 1667)
Knight, C., *The Dutch in the Medway* (Chatham; no date)
Kort en Bondigh Verhael van't geene in den Oorlogh Tusschen den Koning van Engelant . . . etc. (Amsterdam, 1667)
Lediard, T., *The Naval History of England* (London, 1735)
Lefevre-Pontalis, M. A., *John de Witt* (2 vols., London, 1885)
Lewis, M., *The Navy of Britain* (London, 1948)
London Gazette
  No. 163 (6–10 June 1667)
  No. 164 (10–13 June 1667)

No. 165 (13–17 June 1667)

No. 167 (20–24 June 1667)

No. 198 (7–10 October 1667)

Long, A. G., *Some Things Nearly So: The Dutch Raid on the River Medway June 1667* (Chatham, Production Dept., H.M. Dockyard, 1967)

Macaulay, T. B., *The History of England* (Vol. I, London, 1849)

Mahan, A. T., *The Influence of Sea Power upon History* (London, 1892)

Margoliouth, H. M., *The Poems and Letters of Andrew Marvell* (2 vols., Oxford, 1927)

Mathew, D., *The Naval Heritage* (London, 1945)

Muddiman, J. G., 'The Dutch at Chatham 1667' (in *Notes and Queries* 11 April 1936)

Muller van Brakel, F., '*Cornelis de Witt op de Vloot*' (in *Marineblad*, Den Helder, 1955)

— '*De Tocht naar Chatham slechts half geslaagd*' (in *Marineblad*, Den Helder, 1952)

Ogg, D., *England in the Reign of Charles II* (Oxford, 1956)

Ollard, R., *Man of War: Sir Robert Holmes and the Restoration Navy* (London, 1969)

Oppenheim, M., *A History of the Administration of the Royal Navy* (Vol. I, 1509–1660, London, 1896)

— *Kent, Maritime History* (in *Victoria County History of Kent*, Vol. II, London, 1926)

— *The Naval Tracts of Sir William Monson* (5 vols., Navy Records Society, 1902–14)

Oudendijk, J. K., *Johan de Witt en de Zeemacht* (Amsterdam, 1944)

Peace Concluded and Trade Revived in an Honourable Peace betwixt the English and Dutch (London, 1667)

Penn, G., *Memorials of the Professional Life and Times of Sir William Penn* (Vol. II, London, 1833)

Pepys, S., *Diary* (edited H. B. Wheatley, 3 vols., London, 1923)

Perrin, W. G., *The Autobiography of Phineas Pett* (Navy Records Society, London, 1918)

Piper, D., *Catalogue of Seventeenth Century Portraits in the National Portrait Gallery 1625–1714* (Cambridge, 1963)

Ritter, H. A., '*De Tocht naar Chatham*' (in *Marineblad*, Den Helder, 1928)

Saunders, A. D., *Upnor Castle* (London, H.M.S.O., 1967)

Scheffer, A., *Roemruchte Jaren van Onze Vloot 1665–1666–1667* (Baarn, 1966)

Tanner, J. R., *A Descriptive Catalogue of the Naval Manuscripts in the Pepysian Library at Magdalen College Cambridge* (Vol. I, Navy Records Society, London, 1903)

— *Further Correspondence of Samuel Pepys 1662–1679* (London, 1929)

— *Samuel Pepys and the Royal Navy* (Cambridge, 1920)

Tawney, R. H., *Religion and the Rise of Capitalism* (London, 1944)

Tedder, A. W., *The Navy of the Restoration* (Cambridge, 1916)

Temple, Sir William, *Works* (2 vols., London, 1720)

Ten Raa, F. J. G., and de Bas, F., *Het Staatsche Leger 1568–1795* (Deel V, Breda, 1921)

The Dutch-mens Pedigree (London, 1653)

The English and Dutch Affairs Displayed to the Life (London, 1664)

The Second Dutch War 1665–67 (National Maritime Museum, London, 1967)

Trevelyan, G. M., *English Social History* (London, 1948)

Vale, V., *Clarendon, Coventry and the Sale of Naval Offices 1660–68* (in *Cambridge Historical Journal*, Vol. XII, No. 2, 1956)

Vere, F., *Salt in Their Blood: The Lives of the Famous Dutch Admirals* (London, 1955)

Vondel: Volledige Dichterwerken en Oorspronkelijk Prosa Verzorgd en Ingeleid door Albert Verweg (Amsterdam, 1937)

Warburton, E., *Memoirs of Prince Rupert and the Cavaliers* (Vol. III, London, 1849)

Warner, O., *Hero of the Restoration: A Life of General George Monck I^st Duke of Albemarle, K.G.* (London, 1936)

Wilcox, L. A., *Mr. Pepys's Navy* (London, 1966)

Wilson, C., *England's Apprenticeship 1603–1763* (London, 1965)

— *Holland and Britain* (London; n.d.)

— *Profit and Power: A Study of England and the Dutch Wars* (London, 1957)

Wortley, Hon. J. Stuart, *Memoirs of George Monk Duke of Albemarle, translated from the French of M. Guizot* (London, 1838)

Index